What people a

T0007410

Mindfulness and Me

Markoff's informal and approachable style of writing demystifies mindfulness and provides readers with a clear understanding of why and how to engage in activities that reduce stress and promote well-being, tranquility, and contentment. I urge everyone to give mindfulness—and Markoff's handbook—a try.
Carolyn Knight, MSW, Ph.D., Professor Emeritus of Social Work University of Maryland Baltimore County; author of *Introduction to Working with Adult Survivors of Childhood Trauma: Strategies and Techniques for Helping Professionals*.

The concept of mindfulness can be intimidating and overwhelming for some beginners, as well as difficult to grasp at times of chaos. Markoff's *Mindfulness and Me* is an encouraging guide to self-care and provides inspiration for living a happier life with a calmer mind.
Amy West, LCPC, M.S., Psychotherapist treating mental health and substance use disorders since 2018

Mindfulness and Me

A Practical Guide for Living

Mindfulness and Me

A Practical Guide for Living

Kira M. Markoff, LCSW-C

Winchester, UK
Washington, USA

JOHN HUNT PUBLISHING

First published by O-Books, 2023
O-Books is an imprint of John Hunt Publishing Ltd., 3 East St., Alresford,
Hampshire SO24 9EE, UK
office@jhpbooks.com
www.johnhuntpublishing.com
www.o-books.com

For distributor details and how to order please visit the 'Ordering' section on our website.

Text copyright: Kira M. Markoff, LCSW-C 2022

ISBN: 978 1 80341 222 1
978 1 80341 223 8 (ebook)
Library of Congress Control Number: 2022934747

A CIP catalogue record for this book is available from the British Library.

Design: Matthew Greenfield

UK: Printed and bound by CPI Group (UK) Ltd, Croydon, CR0 4YY
Printed in North America by CPI GPS partners

We operate a distinctive and ethical publishing philosophy in all areas of our business, from our global network of authors to production and worldwide distribution.

Contents

It is with unending gratitude that I dedicate this book to all the teachers in my life. You help me see my strengths and push me to be better. My first lesson in balance. Thank you.

Introduction

My mom always told me, "There is nothing new under the sun." Which I later learned was actually my mom quoting Ecclesiastes – a book in the Old Testament of the Christian Bible – because that's just what my parents did (and still do). What she meant is that there really are no new ideas, and if you look through history, you'll see she was right. The same concepts are repeated over and over again by Yogis, Buddhist monks, Japanese Zen practitioners, Roman Stoics and Greek philosophers, French philosophers, and even Freud and his descendants in modern psychology. There are just certain truths about life that reappear throughout time and place, and that's what this book is about. I am not claiming to have invented some new way of thinking or interacting with the world. This book is about taking the beautiful practices, explanations, and points of view from all the wonderful places in history to create a practical and relatable guidebook which can be used by anyone regardless of age, religion, ethnicity, or socioeconomic status. This book is possible only through the clarity, insight, and practice of all those who have come before me. May it help you see further than the knowledge it contains.

"If I see further than others, it is by standing upon the shoulders of giants." ~ Sir Isaac Newton in a letter to Robert Hooke dated 1675 (1).

Buddhist monk Thich Nhat Hanh once told a story about the invention of shoes that went something like this: A long time ago in a kingdom somewhere beautiful, there lived a king who loved his daughter, the princess, very much. This was a time before shoes existed, so everyone walked barefooted everywhere they went. One beautiful spring day, the princess was out for a walk and stubbed her toe. She was in such pain. She hopped on one foot, cradling her wounded foot, until she fell over. The

1

village people nearby began to laugh and point. Humiliated, the princess ran to her father, the King, in tears. The King was so distressed at his daughter's suffering that he called his court advisor and demanded that the entire kingdom be covered in leather so that everywhere the princess walked, she would be protected and would not hurt herself again. The advisor was quite concerned at this command because he knew how expensive this would be for the kingdom and how unrealistic it would turn out to be. He took some time to think and came back to the King with a solution. He said to the King, "What if, instead of covering the kingdom in leather, we fashion some leather to bind around the princess's foot. That way, no matter where she goes and what she steps on, she will be protected." The King was pleased by this, and the first leather shoe was made for the princess who walked peacefully throughout the kingdom thereafter.

You may have guessed that this story is not the true history of shoes. The purpose of this story is to show the way that mindfulness acts as a protection against a world that is full of pain and suffering. There are so many things in this world that are hurtful: other peoples' words, our own thoughts, unavoidable experiences, empathy and compassion for the suffering of others. It can be overwhelming. Mindfulness is a practice of protecting yourself from identifying with the experience. Someone says something unkind, and we don't take it personally because we have the mindfulness to remember they are speaking out of their own suffering. We think a negative thought about ourselves, and we are not wounded because we are in mindfulness (sometimes translated as remembering) and know that our thoughts are not true to reality. We are angry and are not hurt by our anger nor do we hurt others in our anger because we have the mindfulness to breathe with our anger and recognize it as a temporary visitor clouding our judgment.

I often paraphrase a quote from Jon Kabat-Zinn and

say to people, "When you stop trying to make something special happen, you realize that something special is already happening". There is a popular myth that mindfulness and meditation is something mystical and magical, and that is partly correct. There is a magic in simply letting things be as they are. There is magic in breathing. There is mystery in being in tune with our own experience and with nature. The only way to experience the true gifts that meditation and mindfulness have to offer is by setting aside your beliefs and assumptions about what you think it's *supposed* to be.

A Brief History of Meditation

You're not alone if your first thought when you read the word 'meditation' is an Asian man in orange robes sitting in a monastery in silence for hours on end. You are partly correct. Meditation is the translation of a Sanskrit word *Smrti*. Sanskrit is an Ancient Indian language, so you see it a lot with original Hindu, Buddhist, and Yogic writings because they all came from India a few thousand years ago. Smrti (meditation) was a practice for improving mental clarity, focus, and emotional stability among other things. Unfortunately, the everyday practicality of this mental exercise is lost in cultural translation and meditation became associated with Buddhism as a religious custom.

I say 'unfortunately', not because there is anything wrong with being a Buddhist, but because a lot of people assume that meditation is not for them simply because it is seen as a Buddhist religious practice. Buddhism was originally developed as a way of understanding and reducing human suffering and meditation was a primary way to do just that. Meditation is also a core practice in other religions and life philosophies such as Zen, Tao, Yoga, Hinduism, and – believe it or not – Christianity. For all of these life philosophies and religions, the major tenets include kindness, patience, generosity, compassion, nonattachment, peace, and simplicity.

Meditation was developed as a tool. It was never intended that the goal of meditating would be to be able to meditate. The purpose of meditating is to become better at living. Meditation is a way to cultivate relaxation, inner peace, mental clarity, focus and concentration, emotional stability, kindness and compassion, simplicity, and mastery over cravings and habitual patterns of reacting. These ideals are not exclusive to any culture or religion. They apply to every person in every occupation and in every stage of life. The history of meditation is that it was developed as a way to improve lives and relieve suffering but through misunderstanding and wrong perceptions, it was lost to many people. The truth always reveals itself if one is willing to see it.

A Note on How to Use This Book

I came up with the idea for this book after reading a research study reporting that after eight weeks of daily mindful meditation practices, people showed decreased activity in the fear center of their brain. The fear center of the brain (the amygdala) is also responsible for other similar emotions like stress, anxiety, worry, and even anger. After reading that I thought, 'what a wonderful idea to give people a guidebook to lead them through eight weeks to a less fearful, less stressed out, and less angry brain'. Here are some ways to use this book, and a few words of warning.

Pop culture is spreading the myth that meditation only holds positive or desired emotional and cognitive (a fancy word for thought) experiences. That is not true. Mindful meditation is a chance to be more intentional in your life. These practices help you to become available for the full range of human experiences. That is difficult. It's uncomfortable. I highly recommend working with a trained professional – yoga instructor, meditation teacher, religious leader, therapist, mentor, etc – to support and guide you through difficult emotional experiences. If you are a person who has experienced trauma or if you have a mental health disorder such as depression, anxiety, borderline personality disorder, a substance use disorder, bipolar disorder, or any other, then it may be necessary for you to do this work with the help of a teacher. The purpose of a meditation practice is to stop efforting, to stop fighting. If a practice feels wrong to you, then don't do it. It's really that simple. You gain nothing by fighting.

That being said, there is value in sitting with discomfort. There is a difference between forcing yourself to stay with a practice that is not right for you versus sitting in the discomfort of a practice. Be intentional. You are in control. This book is merely a guide. I have laid out 56 activities as daily practices across eight weeks organized into topics. I organized them based on my own personal experience, education, and what made the most sense to me. This might not be the best way for you. Let yourself take the lead. Skip around. Do them out of order. Don't do some. Do some twice or even three times. Change the times or number of breath cycles. Be curious and let yourself have fun. Sometimes being led is nice, too, and if that's where you're at, then I'm honored to lead you. The choice is yours. This is your life. Live it.

Meditation Postures

Traditionally meditation is practiced sitting, standing, laying down, or walking. You're welcome to practice in whatever way feels best to you. Over the last few thousand years practitioners have passed down guidance on posture. Arranging your body in a certain way has no impact on the benefits of the practice (people disagree with me, but I stand by what I said). The sole purpose is to make sure that your body is comfortable so that it doesn't distract you from your meditation and so that meditating doesn't cause any long-term harm to your body. I'll walk you through how to arrange your body in the traditional way, but feel free to make any adjustments based on what works for your body.

Sitting: Feel free to sit against a wall to help support you. It might feel good to sit up on a cushion or rolled up blanket. Move any excess butt cheek out of the way and make sure that you feel stable, grounded, and balanced on your sits bones (anatomical name: ischial tuberosities). Your legs are crossed in front of you with your knees wide enough that one foot is directly in front of the other with tops of the feet rotating outwardly toward the ground. Feel both grounded through your tailbone and lifted through the crown of your head. There is a slight activation in your core and your shoulders are relaxed. Your elbows hang directly below your shoulders which keeps your shoulders from becoming misaligned. Your hands fall somewhere along your thighs. It's more important that your elbows are aligned with relaxed shoulders than to have any particular hand placement. In yoga, this pose is called Sukhasana which means easy seat. Many people will say that lotus pose is the optimal seated meditation pose; however, without proper guidance and practice, you're likely to blow out a hip or a knee if you try lotus, so I recommend sticking with easy seat.

Standing: Start with your feet about shoulder width apart. Feel balanced and grounded. Notice a slight activation in your calves and inner thighs. There is a lifting in the front of your body – through the core, chest, and head. Chin might tuck slightly so the crown of your head is level, and the back of the neck is lengthened. The back body is grounding down – relaxed shoulders and out through the heels. Arms are down the side of your body with palms facing forward. Fingers are spread apart and active.

Laying down: Essentially standing only the ground is underneath your whole body instead of just your feet. Feet are shoulder width apart perhaps relaxed, so the toes are pointed outward. Relax through the legs, back, and abdomen. Shoulders are down away from the ears. Chin is slightly tucked so the back of the neck isn't crunched. Arms are down along the sides with palms facing up. The distance between the body and the hands isn't important, so just do whatever is comfortable. If you have sensation in the lower back feel free to bend your knees and plant your feet. Knees can either be in line with hips or you can take your feet wide and have your knees leaned into each other. Alternatively, you could create a diamond with your legs with knees wide and soles of the feet together. Try the options and see what feels best for you. It might be something different each day, and that's okay.

Week 1

Presence

I am a mental health therapist by day and meditation teacher and psychology PhD student by night. A real-life batman I suppose. I was talking once to a client about her goals, and she said to me, "I want to be an active participant in my life". This really struck me. With her permission, I've been using it ever since. Think about it, can you really say that you're an active participant in your life? In order to participate, you have to be there. You have to be in the moment. The now. Life happens in the current moment and if you're somewhere else – your thoughts, memories, fears, future, stresses – then you're missing it.

Life moves on without you. How many times have you said good morning to someone without making eye contact? Been driving, and you realize you don't even remember the last 10 miles of the trip? Been lying in bed with your partner and you're on your phone and not even consciously aware that they're there with you? These are moments of your life that you are not going to get back. All too often it takes a drastic event like a death or a divorce for people to realize how much of their life and relationship passed by on autopilot without much notice. Consider this your opportunity to learn that lesson now. Before it becomes painful.

Every beautiful and wonderful thing happens in the present moment. Some painful things happen in the present, but honestly, a lot of our pain and suffering comes from old stories, thoughts, fears about the future, and clinging to some expectation or situation. Art is created in the present moment. Hugs, kisses, and holding hands happen in the present moment. Smells, sights, sounds, and tastes are all present moment experiences. Being in the now also gives you the power to make changes. You can plan and prepare all you want, but it takes being in the moment and deciding to actually do something different in order to make a change in your life. Mindfulness is a practice of empowerment. It all starts here.

1.1

Paying Attention

When people think of being present, or even mindfulness in general, usually what they are thinking about is paying attention. This is part of it, but by no means all of it. Presence is paying attention plus. Attention plus open-mindedness. Attention plus kindness. Attention plus non-defensiveness. The point is, presence is not a synonym for attention, but attention is a skill that we have to practice. Attention is basically two brain functions: attending to an object and ignoring anything that isn't that. Let's say that you want to be present to the wind in the trees, to a conversation, to a hug, or to an emotion. Your attention is like a flashlight. You can choose where to direct it, so you direct it to the object. The problem is, your brain will do that willingly for like .3 seconds and then it's like 'okay, took that in, what's next?' and your attention continues to dart around from thing to thing, distraction to distraction, internal story to internal story. Ignoring distractions is new for your brain. It's difficult and it goes against what your brain does naturally.

The practice of presence is not about fighting your brain. Mindful meditation is not a practice of struggling. Quite the opposite. Mindfulness and meditation are practices of not efforting, of not fighting, of gently guiding. A lot of people think that meditation is about not getting distracted. There is this myth in pop culture that to be meditating 'correctly' your mind has to be blank or you have to be able to focus for 15, 30, or 60 minutes at a time without a single distraction. This could not be further from the truth. Meditation is a practice of learning to get distracted and come back to the object of your meditation. Imagine distractions like ripples on the surface of a lake. Wind exists. Currents exist. Birds land on the lake and people throw in rocks. There are ripples. That's just the nature of being a lake. We don't say, 'in order to be a peaceful lake, you must get rid of all your ripples'. Can you accept that having distractions is not something to get rid of, but just a natural part of being a person?

PRACTICE

Tip of the Nose

1. If you're just starting, it's good to find a place with few distractions to make this easier for yourself as you're getting used to the process. With enough practice, you could probably do this in the middle of a rowdy sports game or maybe even during a pause in a heated conversation.
2. It's best to close your eyes so your eyes aren't taking up your attention space.
3. Shine your internal flashlight at the tip of your nose – your nostrils to be exact.
4. Tune in to the feeling of air entering your nostrils on the inhale and leaving your nostrils on the exhale.
5. Ignore everything else.
6. You can do this for as long as you want, but I recommend at least 5-10 rounds of breath.
7. It's normal to be distracted – how softly can you redirect the attention? How easy can you make this?
8. Take a moment when you're done to let your attention wander throughout your body and notice any changes.

1.2

Sound

I was teaching a meditation class once and someone (my own mother, can you believe it?) asked me why meditate? She said, "I understand how to do it, but I don't know why I'm doing it." If meditation were a snack, it would be apples with peanut butter – both delicious and nutritious. The practice of mindful meditation is enjoyable and transferable. To sit is enjoyable. To breathe is enjoyable. It is pleasant to wash your hands, to listen to the wind through the trees, and to smell fresh coffee in the morning. We can all use a little more enjoyment in our lives. We exist so much on auto pilot going from this thing to that thing without letting ourselves take in the pleasant things all around us. You might be in a rush to drive from work to home and spend the whole drive thinking about how tired you are, what you have to do when you get home, or processing the workday. You've missed the beautiful colored skies, the funny cow shaped cloud, the rainbow, the pitter patter of the rain, and so much more. Imagine spending your drive enjoying the sights and sounds rather than indulging your thoughts which, let's be honest, are probably more like an exhausted hamster on a wheel than anything productive.

If the opportunity to enjoy more of your life isn't enough for you then you might enjoy the generalization of skills that mindful meditation has to offer. Your brain works with patterns. Every time you do something new, you're creating a new connection in your brain's neural pathways. Each time you practice that skill, you strengthen the connection and make it easier for your brain to do. Different meditation practices focus on different skills (kindness, compassion, relaxation/ calmness, breath control, focus/concentration, understanding, nonjudgment, open-mindedness, and so forth); however, all meditation practices improve your ability to be more intentional with your life. All meditation practices work on giving you the power to make a conscious and active choice rather than being dragged around by your habits, cultural conditioning, thought patterns, previous learning, expectations, and emotional reactions. Imagine being in the middle of an argument and noticing you're angry, taking a breath, and making the choice to recognize the other person is stressed or insecure. How might that change your interaction? Imagine feeling anxious and making the decision to practice a breathing technique to relax your body and talk yourself through it. Imagine being able to not act on your own fears or anger. Imagine not self-sabotaging. These are the gifts of meditation.

PRACTICE

Meditating on Sound

1. Find a place to sit/stand/lie down and set your timer for five minutes.
2. Close your eyes and breathe in and out fully for about three cycles of breath.
3. Focus only on the things you can hear.
4. Ignore everything else.
5. Avoid the temptation to label, figure out, or judge the sounds, just let them float in and out like waves passing through your ears.
6. Simply Observe.
7. Release any tension. Straining. Holding.
8. Challenge yourself to focus on sounds close by then sounds far away.
9. Whenever your attention wanders, gently guide it back to the experience of listening.
10. When your timer goes off, give yourself a moment to scan your body and notice the effects of your practice.

1.3

Sight

You are not on guard against distractions. The purpose of meditating is not to beat away distractions with the almighty power of your attention. Your ultimate goal in a meditation is to be so entirely focused on the object of your meditation that the distractions fall away naturally, and when they do arise, they are softly swept away as you gently guide your attention back to your meditation. The object of your meditation is like an anchor. Your mind is an ocean with waves washing you this way or that. It's easy to get swept away and sometimes it can even feel like you might drown. Rest easy, little boat. Meditation is an anchor that will hold you steady in the face of even the roughest storms.

Rest easy, little boat. Give yourself permission to enjoy this practice. Be intentional. We look at things all day long. We usually aren't even consciously aware of our eyes – what are they choosing to look at? What are they ignoring? It might be enjoyable for you to take a moment and be grateful for your eyes and the hard work that they do all day long to keep you safe and help you go about your day. Some things are pleasant to look at and some things are not. This is just a fact of life. Right now, you have a choice of what to look at. Choose something enjoyable. There is no need to make life harder or more unpleasant for yourself than it already is. As you complete this practice, challenge yourself to look at the object with fresh eyes as if you are seeing it for the first time. Notice everything. Resist the urge to create stories or *think* about the object. Just look at it. Notice the lines and the colors.

PRACTICE

Looking with Fresh Eyes

1. Find a place to sit/stand/lie and set your timer for three or five minutes.
2. Choose something pleasant to look at (painting, person, leaf, your own hand).
3. Allow yourself to be fully immersed in the experience of looking.
4. If your mind starts to wander or tries to create stories about what you're looking at, softly redirect your attention only to experience what you're seeing.
5. When your timer goes off, allow yourself a few moments to notice the effects of your practice. Feel free to journal about your experience if the mood strikes you.

1.4

Smell

Freshly baked cookies. A bouquet of flowers. The sidewalk after a summer rainstorm. Can you smell it? If you're like most people, then the answer is yes. Our sense of smell is so tied to our memories, and guess what? That relationship goes both ways. A smell can throw you back into a memory just as easily as a memory can feel so real that you smell it. There are so many smells all around us every day, but our brains ignore them! Our brain only pays attention to new things or things that it has coded as important to our safety or functioning. It's time to teach our brain that being present and enjoying this moment *is* important to our safety and functioning. Giving time and attention to your sense of smell is a wonderful way to bring yourself into the present moment and bask in it.

Five senses grounding is becoming really popular in mental health therapy. It's the practice of using the five senses (taste, touch, smell, hearing, and sight) to reground, recenter, and relax people who are stressed, anxious, or even in the middle of a panic attack. Honestly, I feel like smell is kind of overlooked here. It's the unsung hero of the senses. I bet, if you had to pick a sense to get rid of, you'd probably choose smell, wouldn't you? But think about all the wonderful times you've had with your nose. All of the times you've hugged someone and just breathed in so deeply because it feels so good. We are so quick to give up things that bring us enjoyment in place of things we see as 'necessary for functioning'. I'm here to tell you that you don't have to choose. Even more than that, I'm here to tell you that enjoying your life actually makes you a more productive person! The story that you have to choose to either enjoy your life or be productive is a *lie*. So, if you believe that your life has a purpose, stop and smell the roses!

Stop, Drop, and Smell

1. Get something with a smell that you really enjoy (examples: coffee, tea, freshly baked pastries, perfume, lotion, essential oil, dirt, a loved one's hoodie or blanket, a piece of fruit).
2. Set your timer for three minutes.
3. Close your eyes and breathe in for as long as you can – drinking in all the nuances of smell.
4. Let it surround you and fill you up.
5. Exhale.
6. Take another long, slow inhale. And another. And another.
7. Allow yourself a few moments after your timer goes off to enjoy the effects of your practice.

1.5

Taste

Taste means eat, and eat means to consume, right? Literally, the word 'consume' means to take in. You take in food and drink, that's true. But you also take in other things, like books, movies, social media posts, other people's words and attitudes. You consume music, ways of thinking about things, ways of doing things, beliefs about success and about yourself. You even consume the emotions of other people. Everything that you perceive using your five senses is consumption. Well, 'you are what you eat' they say. You don't eat donuts and drink soda all day and expect to feel fresh and energetic, so why do you watch endless TikToks or spend time around people who make you feel bad about yourself and expect to feel passionate and motivated? Mindfulness means being in remembrance. Remembering that we are affected by everything around us. Mindfulness might be our shoes, but just because you're wearing shoes doesn't mean you should go running across hot coals or stepping on rusty nails. It's important to be aware of the things you're consuming so that you recognize the effects.

My sisters and I used to compare books to food. A book that was kind of boring but good for you might be kale, while a romantic comedy might be cotton candy. It's okay to eat some cotton candy here and there. It's delicious and it hits the spot at a carnival. The problem comes when you go through life only eating cotton candy and not even realizing it! The purpose of mindfulness is not to create strict rules for yourself or always to make the healthy decision. It's about being aware of the reality of how things are and giving yourself the power to choose. Are you eating cotton candy out of habit or because you sincerely want cotton candy? Are you watching TikTok because you're zoning out of your life and avoiding reality, or because you're genuinely enjoying a particular channel or video? Be aware of what you're consuming. Take in with intention. Savor your life experiences.

PRACTICE

Taste Meditation

1. Ask yourself this question: 'What do I really want to taste right now?' Honor the answer. If it's candy, let it be candy. If it's carrots, let it be carrots.
2. Sit down in a quiet space with your food.
3. Breathe in and out before placing it in your mouth.
4. Experience.
5. Notice the flavors, texture, the way it feels in your mouth.
6. Let yourself be entirely in the experience for as long as it lasts.
7. Challenge yourself to slow down as much as feels comfortable. There's no need to rush from place to place. This is your time to be.

1.6

Touch

I remember sitting in church as a kid, and my dad got up to give a lesson and he said, 'We live in a throw away world'. It seemed like everyone kind of gasped and got a little confused. His point was that people in today's world can sometimes be so quick to just give up on things. It's damaged, too hard, not what we wanted, so we just throw it away. This being a church service, his point was that God didn't do that with us. Whether you're Christian or not, the point stands. We do live in a throw away world. We live in a world of disposable phones, plates, water bottles, and people. Relationship too hard? Break up with them. Someone said something insensitive to you? Cut them out. Our culture lives in the delusion that everything and everyone is replaceable. Plain and simple that is untrue. Not everything is fun, fast, and easy. Life is about balance. It's true that sometimes relationships need to end and sometimes you're safer if you don't associate with someone. It's also true that relationships take a lot of hard work and sometimes it's better to sit in the difficulty than to just end it so it's not hard anymore.

When we touch something, we connect with it. The transfer goes both ways. We affect it. It affects us. Skin-to-skin contact with a loved one actually releases chemicals in your brain that make you feel good. They've done studies on the effects of skin-to-skin contact between a mother and a newborn baby. Touch is important to our well-being. Nothing is going to feel good and be easy all the time. Our conditioning is that when something doesn't feel good then that means we need to get rid of it. Mindfulness is the remembrance that something can be worthwhile and beautiful even if it feels uncomfortable or painful at times. Mindful meditation can also help give us the clarity to see if something is worthwhile and painful or if it's destructive and needs to be changed. Emotions, urgency, and fears cloud our vision and make things confusing. Use your meditation practice to quiet the waves and allow yourself to see things for how they truly are.

PRACTICE

Connecting through Touch

1. Find a calm place to sit, stand, or lie down.
2. Close your eyes.
3. Breathe in and out three times.
4. Like a flashlight, direct your attention to each place that connects with a surface and let it rest there for a full cycle of breath.
5. Notice the connection coming in through your feet, legs, sits bones (polite way of saying butt), maybe your whole back.
6. Observe the sensation of body against surface. Notice any words that come up and just let them be. There is no need to change anything.
7. Let yourself release into the feeling of connection.
8. Breathe in and out three times to end.
9. Allow yourself a moment to feel the effects of your practice.

1.7

Awareness Journaling

This is the final day in the week of presence practices. It seems an appropriate time for a small discussion of the difference between mindfulness and meditation. Many people use them interchangeably and there's no reason to get overly concerned about the difference, but it's helpful to know. Mindfulness is where the rubber meets the road. Mindfulness, sometimes translated as being in remembrance, is being aware, in the moment, with openness, serenity, and curiosity which is, perhaps, cultivated during a meditation practice. Mindfulness is for every moment. Mindfulness is remembering to breathe slowly and smoothly when someone is angry. Mindfulness is recognizing that the cashier's bad attitude is affecting you, giving you the power to let it stop affecting you. Mindfulness is living your life in the pilot's seat rather than on autopilot.

Meditation is the practice that gets you there. Humans can't just wake up, decide to run a marathon, and then run a marathon. Well, life is a marathon. Meditation is the set of practices that hone your skills to be kind, compassionate, calm, clear-minded, attentive, and emotionally non-reactive. Meditation practices are times intentionally set aside to practice. It can be walking, standing, sitting, or lying down. A meditation practice meets you where you are. It is enjoyable and best practiced in a calm and quiet space. Put another way: meditation practices set you up to live a mindful life.

PRACTICE

Awareness Journaling

1. Get paper and pen. Go to a calm and quiet space.
2. Set your timer for five minutes.
3. Breathe in and out three times.
4. Finish this sentence: I am aware of...
5. Write. As many things as you want. As many sentences as you want.
6. If you have extra time, feel free to re-read what you wrote or simply sit in silence.
7. Allow yourself a few moments to observe the effects of your practice.

Week 2

Breathing Techniques

One of the things that I love best about mindful meditation is that there are so many parallels to Western psychology and neurobiology which is the study of neurons, the cells that make up the brain, spinal cord, and peripheral nervous system. A lot of calming practices begin with breathing, whether they label themselves as mindfulness practices or not. We tell kids to take a few deep breaths, take a breather, or even count to ten which we all know is code for stop and breathe. There's a scientific reason that this works. Basically, your brain is split into two types of functioning: essential and non-essential. Essential parts of the brain regulate the stress response, eating, breathing, sex-drive, and so forth. Non-essential functions are the ones like problem solving, planning, and abstract thinking. I know these don't sound like non-essential functions, but the categories are based on what is necessary to maintain life.

You may have noticed that the stress response is part of the 'essential functions' family of brain activities. This is really important. When your brain identifies something as potentially dangerous for you then it activates the stress response which, for all intents and purposes, shuts down the non-essential functioning so that all energy is diverted to the essential functions. Functions like problem-solving, open-mindedness, nonjudgment, and compassion go offline. Muscles tense. Heart rate increases. Breathing becomes shallow and fast. Also, your digestive system and immune system stop functioning normally which is why digestive issues and sickness are commonly linked to stress. All of these things happen automatically because bodies are pretty cool like that. The stress response is pretty helpful for running away from a lion or lifting a car off a baby. Not so useful when your partner gets upset and – oopsie! – all your rational thinking goes offline. Here's where it gets really cool.

I said all of it happens automatically, and that's true. The cool thing about breathing is that it's only partially automatic. We also have control over our breathing. The stress response is a chain reaction both to get it going and to get it to stop. When the breathing returns to normal – slows down, becomes deeper, smoothes out – that signals the rest of the body that the stress response is no longer needed. Heart rate slows down. Muscles relax. Stress hormones are no longer released to circulate throughout the body. Perhaps most importantly, the rest of the brain functions come back online. This normal functioning is often referred to as the 'rest and digest' mode. The breath is the direct key into the body's stress response. It's a hack to retrain the brain how to respond to different situations in life. This week takes you through seven breathing exercises to switch your body from stressed out to rest and digest.

2.1

Dirgha

Dirgha is a Sanskrit word that is usually translated as 'long' or 'lengthy'. It's a way to slow down the breath and actively engage different muscle groups to bring attention to various parts of a breath cycle. Dirgha is a really common breath practice in yoga and meditation classes and is sometimes just called a 'belly breath' or '3-part breath'. I've heard it said that in the upper part of the lungs are receptors for the stress response while in the lower part of the lungs there are receptors for the rest and digest functioning. Therefore, by redirecting the breath to the lower part of the lungs you actually stimulate the switch into relaxed nervous system functioning. To be totally honest, I'm not sure if that's scientifically valid or not. There's a lot in yoga philosophy that western science has yet to verify but you ask yourself, does that really matter? Does it matter if there are parasympathetic neuron receptors in the lower part of the lungs? That's up to you. I say, if it works then it works regardless of the reason why.

The three body part groups of a dirgha practice are belly, ribs, and chest. You start by breathing in and feeling your belly expand. You can envision a balloon filling and emptying. You can even place your hands on your belly to feel the rise and fall. Do this about three times or until you have a good sense of what it feels like. On the next inhale, fill your belly then continue breathing in and let your breath fill up your ribs. Notice the rib cage flare out, maybe seeing them as gills of a fish. Feel free to move your hands to your ribcage to help guide your breath here. Exhale, ribs contract then belly empties. Inhale, fill the belly. Fill the ribs. Continue for three cycles of breath. On this inhale, fill the belly completely. Let the air move up to flare the ribs. Once the rib space is filled, allow the air to continue moving upward to lift the chest. Again, you can move your hands to your chest to feel the rise and fall. Exhale. Chest falls. Ribs close. Belly empties. Inhale. Belly fills. Ribs expand. Chest rises. Some people find it helpful to envision a zipper opening from the bottom of the belly to the top of the chest with each inhale then zipping closed from chest to bottom of the belly on the exhale. You could also use the image of a wave coming up to the shore then moving out to sea. Be curious and explore what works best for you. It's normal for this practice to be difficult at first. After all, you've never asked your body to breathe this way before. With time and practice, this will become easier and smoother.

PRACTICE

Dirgha

1. Go to a calm, peaceful space.
2. Choose three of the following body positions: standing, sitting, lying on your back, lying on your belly, lying with your back on the floor and your legs up on the wall or a chair, and lying on your side.
3. If you choose to lie on your side, consider doing both left and right side as two different positions.
4. Complete five rounds of dirgha breath in each of the three positions.
5. Be curious about the way the breath feels different in each body shape.
6. Allow yourself some time to notice the effects of your practice.

2.2

Box Breath

This is one of those breath practices that people do without even intending it as mindfulness or a mini meditation. Actually, divers use this practice to increase their lung capacity for deeper and longer dives. Therapists often recommend this practice to patients suffering with anxiety disorder. Much as I support the spread of mindfulness practices, I do believe even the most well-intentioned advice can be problematic sometimes. For example, some people have really bad experiences with box breath because they're doing it the way that someone told them to and it made them feel worse. Typically, I've heard it with people who have anxiety, and they try box breath, and it makes them feel more anxious. If this is your experience, then you've come to the right place. Forget the rules. There are no real rules in breathing practices. It's all guidelines and anyone who's telling you differently is operating on a wrong belief. Okay, maybe there's one rule, and that's to keep breathing. If you don't, you will die. This rule is really just for your safety.

Box breath is traditionally taught as inhale – hold – exhale – hold each to a count of four and repeated for several cycles. Depending on who's teaching it, the counts are different, and they may eliminate one or both of the holds. The mere fact that there's so much diversity in how people teach it should be enough to tell you that the rules are made up. It doesn't matter if you hold for a count of four or fourteen. What matters is that you find it relaxing and enjoyable. Breathing is enjoyable. So often we do things because we're told to do them a certain way or because we think we're supposed to do them a certain way, and we never even stop to reflect if it even works for us. You're feeling rushed to get married because our culture says you're supposed to get married, but if you were to pause and reflect on it, you might realize that you're actually content with your life as it is. You put parmesan on your spaghetti because that's the way it's always been done, but if you tried it, you might find that you actually prefer pepper jack on your pasta. This is your personal invitation to say, 'screw the rules!' and do what works for you. Change the counts. Eliminate one or both of the holds. Do each round differently. The choice is yours!

Box Breath

1. Find a calm, quiet place.
2. Close your eyes.
3. Breathe in for a count of four.
4. Hold for a count of four.
5. Breathe out for a count of four.
6. Hold for a count of four.
7. Repeat for five complete cycles.
8. Breathe normally for a few rounds and notice the effects of your practice.
9. Yes. These directions were a test. Alter them as desired.

2.3

Ujjayi

Ujjayi (pronounced – Oo-Jai or Oo-Jai-EE) is translated as the one who is victorious. In yoga practices it is often called victorious breath or ocean breath. Breathing practice is one of the eight limbs of yoga, Pranayama. Yoga simply means connection and the eight limbs of yoga bring about connection in mind, body, and spirit. Prana is the universal life force which is believed to travel up and down the spine giving life, energy, clarity, passion, and facilitating the connection to self, others, and the universe. Pranayama is the harnessing and movement of the prana so that it can flow freely throughout the body. The belief is that it gets stuck by blockages caused by old stories, wrong beliefs, negativity, and inflexibility – mental, physical, and spiritual. A yoga asana practice (the poses) is designed to create space, strengthen the body, establish balance, and increase flexibility. Breath is the bridge between mind and body. When we are fully aware of our breath then our mind and our body are united.

Ujjayi is a beautiful practice for beginning to experience the singularity of mind and body through breathwork. It is called ocean breath because the sound that it makes is like waves of the ocean. It requires control over the muscles in your belly and your throat. It's a pretty forceful out breath and engaging the muscles in your stomach can be really empowering if you let it be. I don't want to spoil too much for our week seven discussion, but in yogic philosophy your stomach is the seat of power and strength. This is probably why this is called victorious breath. When you're practicing Ujjayi, challenge yourself to feel powerful. Let the feeling of victory fill you up and empower you. You are a warrior.

PRACTICE

Victorious Breath

1. Find a quiet place to sit comfortably.
2. Close your eyes.
3. Breathe in fully.
4. On your exhale, open your mouth in a 'ha' as if you were trying to fog up a mirror.
5. With the same throat constriction, suck in air through your mouth.
6. Do this two or three times until you feel comfortable.
7. Simply close your mouth and breathe through your nose, making the same sound.
8. Use your stomach muscles to help create a smooth flow of breath in and out.
9. Notice the sound, like waves crashing against a rock cliff.
10. Feel strong.
11. Continue for 5-8 rounds of breath.
12. Breathe normally for a while. Give yourself time to notice the effects of your practice

This one can be a little challenging at first, so give yourself time for your body to learn what you're asking it to do

2.4

Bhramari Breath

Bhramari breath is also called bumble bee breath, named for the sound you create by practicing it. Bumble bee breath is breath work that brings in another of the eight limbs of yoga – pratyahara. Pratyahara is the practice of turning off your sensory perception. The idea is that your brain is busy all day every day trying to take in and make sense of information from the outside world and it does not leave enough awareness to go inside. There is no energy or space to connect inwardly. Have you ever wondered why you turn down the radio when you're trying to find a particular house number while driving? Or, why you get irritable if you're trying to pay attention to too many things? Or even why children with autism have tantrums with loud noises, bright lights, or just at the feel of certain clothes? All five sensory organs are taking in information all the time and it's the brain's job to process and filter it so that it makes sense, and our behavior is appropriate for the situation. Sometimes it's just too much.

There's actually a term for when your brain is overwhelmed by outside information. It's called being overstimulated. Every piece of outside information is called a stimulus, so when you have too much stimulation then you are overstimulated. Bhramari breath has two purposes: to reduce stimulation and to connect inwardly. You see, all sensory information (seeing, hearing, tasting, feeling, and smelling) is the brain receiving information about the outside world. As humans, we also have the ability to feel what's going on inside our bodies, which is pretty cool! A lot of us haven't really developed our 'inner eye', and it's really important for creating balance and well-being. You are important. It's important for you to be aware of what's going on inside of you. Thus, we have Bhramari. A word of caution: some people find this practice increases their anxiety. If this is the case for you, make the decision if you want to continue the practice or not. Remember, the benefit of practicing comes from the relaxation and centering that it provides, not from the struggle to force yourself to complete a practice.

PRACTICE

Bumble Bee Breath

1. Sit in a quiet, comfortable place.
2. Hold your hands out in front of your face with your palms facing you. Rotate your hands so that your fingertips are pointed at each other (thumbs are pointed up)
3. Place your index and middle fingers over your closed eyes, your fourth fingers over your nostrils, your pinkies at the corner of your mouth, and your thumbs over your ears.
4. Do not block your nostrils completely as you need them to breathe.
5. Holding your hands in this way is both symbolic and functional. Symbolic for nose, feeling, and mouth. Functional for eyes and ears.
6. Inhale fully.
7. As you exhale, make a humming noise. You can experiment with different pitches to see how it feels. Traditionally, higher pitches are energizing, and lower pitches are calming.
8. Relax your shoulders. It's normal for them to creep up by your ears without you noticing.
9. Take 5-8 cycles or until your practice feels complete.
10. Release your hands back to your lap and allow yourself some time to breathe normally and feel the effects of your practice.

2.5

Cooling breath

This practice is wonderful for the summertime or for people who get heated easily (physically or mentally). The cooling breath is also great to use with kids because it's a little silly and also really grounding and calming. There is no rule that says mindful meditation is only for adults, in fact, kids often respond really well to mindfulness practices. Teachers have begun teaching mindfulness in schools and occupational therapists use mindfulness with kid clients to help with emotion regulation and being in tune with the body. Kids tend to like most things that are playful and by that I just mean fun and silly! There's been a lot coming out recently about the value of play not only for kids, but just as much for adults! Play is fun. It's engaging. It gets you out of your head and out of the strict shell you put yourself in.

Play is also vulnerable. It means opening up and being yourself without the protection of decorum. It means being silly even if you get laughed at. It means singing or dancing or making jokes. It means letting your guard down. Play can be scary because it means letting yourself be seen. If you're a person who hasn't played in far too long, then this is a challenge for you. Who is a safe person to play with? Maybe it's a partner, a child, a friend, or other relative. Challenge yourself to be silly with this person. You can even clue them in to what you're doing. Maybe try saying something like, "I'm really trying to loosen up a little, will you be silly with me?" You can do anything! You can sing along to a song in the grocery store or tell a funny joke or talk in a silly voice. You can even start with being whimsical by picking a dandelion as you're walking or putting a leaf in your pocket for the day.

Start where you are, try something, and see how it feels. If that's not mindfulness, then I don't know what is.

PRACTICE

Straw Breathing

1. Find a comfortable, peaceful place to sit, stand, or lie down.
2. Close your eyes.
3. Stick out your tongue and roll it into a straw (if you can).
4. Inhale slowly and steadily through your straw.
5. Notice the sensation of cool air coming in.
6. Place your cool tongue against the top of your mouth while you exhale through your nose.
7. Repeat for 5-8 cycles or until it feels complete.
8. Breathe normally for a while and notice the effects of your practice.

2.6

Lion's breath

Lion's breath is a good time to talk about empathy. Empathy is the willingness (and ability) to understand someone's experience as they see it, especially when it's different from how you see it. Two people can have identical experiences but completely opposite reactions because of their pasts, expectations, current emotional states, and personal preferences. We think that if we've had a similar experience that we are in a better place to understand what someone is going through. This could not be further from the truth and is actually the enemy of true understanding. Assuming that you know what someone is feeling is just as likely to make you stop listening to what they're actually saying as if you were to label what they're saying as 'stupid' or 'unnecessary'.

The only way to truly have empathy for another person is to openly listen to what they're saying. Put aside your expectations for what they're going to say. Put aside your judgments about how they 'should' feel or what a 'normal' feeling would be. Just listen. Let them paint you a picture of their emotional landscape. This is the purest form of love. They are giving you a gift by sharing themself with you. Accept it and treasure it. Even if it's difficult for you to hear. Even if you want to become defensive. Listen to them. Breathe with them. Do not correct them. Deep listening is not the time for correcting a false belief. That could come later if you still think it's necessary. Your only job is to use your mindful breath to create a space where they feel safe to share their life – in all its glory and suffering – with you. I bring this up on lion's breath day because people have really different reactions to this breath practice. Some people – like myself – love it and find it calming and exciting at the same time. It's good to be silly. Some people aren't ready for this level of silliness and just find it uncomfortable. Try it out, if you're ready. Make adjustments as needed. Sometimes it's fun to be silly with others. Sometimes it's nice to do it alone at first while you're trying it out.

PRACTICE

Lion's breath

1. Decide if you want to practice alone or with others.
2. Find a good place for your practice (maybe in front of a mirror).
3. Inhale fully through your nose, filling your belly.
4. On your exhale: open your eyes wide, stick your tongue out and down, and exhale forcefully through your mouth using your core muscle to push the air out.
5. Inhale gently through your nose.
6. Repeat the exhale, perhaps envisioning yourself as a lion when you do so.
7. Continue this for about five cycles or until you feel complete.
8. Breathe normally for several cycles and observe the effects of your practice.

2.7

Alternate Nostril Breath

Alternate nostril breath, nadi shodhana, is a yogic breathing practice whose name means 'to purify the flow'. Traditionally, the practice is believed to clear blocked prana channels and restore balance to the mind and body. The practice consists of using one hand to close off one nostril then the other to actually breathe through one side at a time. If you're into visualizations, it can be great to envision a triangle between the two nostrils and the space between the eyebrows (the third eye). For example, you visualize the breath flowing into the right nostril, up to the third eye as a filter, then out the left nostril. Then repeat in reverse. This is one cycle. If this is a little too out there for you right now, no problem! Just do the breathing technique – or skip it because this is your journey.

The beauty of balance is that everything is right, and good, and welcomed. There is nothing to get rid of because the problem is not that it exists. The issue is the imbalance causing disharmony among the parts of your life. Sadness is right. Depression is sadness out of balance. Prioritizing yourself is right. Self-centeredness is prioritizing yourself out of balance. Accomplishing things is right. Business is accomplishing out of balance. In our world, we have created division and judgment by saying that certain things are right, and their opposites are naturally wrong. Not everyone agrees on the label, but there is a tendency to say, "This is good and that is bad". Imagine a pendulum which swings from extreme to extreme and passes over the middle ground. This shift in mindset happens across generations, cultures, religious sects, and so forth. The goal of nadi shodhana is to restore balance, to bring all aspects of life into harmony with each other.

This is the essence of the yin and yang. Everything together, perfectly balanced, in complete harmony. Consider stress, overwhelm, anxiety as your 'check engine' light telling you that something is out of balance.

Alternate Nostril Breathing

1. Find a quiet, peaceful place and sit comfortably.
2. Rest your left hand in your lap and raise your right hand to your face.
3. You can prop your arm on something if you want. Ensure your shoulders are completely relaxed.
4. Put your index and pointer fingers to the space between your eyebrows or fold them down if you prefer.
5. Exhale completely.
6. Close your right nostril and inhale through your left nostril.
7. Use your ring finger together with your pinkie to close the left nostril briefly before removing your thumb from the right nostril.
8. Exhale through the right nostril. Pause briefly. Inhale through the right nostril.
9. Close both, then open the left nostril for an exhale and an inhale.
10. Complete 5-10 full rounds before ending on a left-side exhale.
11. Breathe normally for a while and allow yourself to notice the effects of your practice.

Week 3

Body-Based Practices

This week is all about mindful meditation practices that are specifically focused on connecting with your body. This is sometimes a really hard thing to do, especially if you're a person who has experienced a trauma, have body dysmorphia, an eating disorder, chronic pain, or even just if you have a difficult relationship with your body. We live in a very intellectual world. A lot of us work at desks staring at phones and computers all day. It can be really easy to forget that you even have a body. Getting back into paying attention to your body – *truly being in your body* – might not sound too appealing to you. Consider that part of the reason you don't like your body is because you haven't spent the time and energy to have positive interactions with it! When's the last time you thought about your right big toe? If you're being honest, it's probably the last time you stubbed your toe!

If you only pay attention to something when it causes problems, then it's easy to think that you don't like the thing. Imagine only paying attention to your friends, your partner, or your kids when they were upset in some way. That would be exhausting and draining for you. You probably wouldn't enjoy being around them very much. That's not their fault though. The solution is to have more positive interactions so that you can enjoy spending time together. In fact, there's an entire style of marital therapy based around the idea that a relationship improves when you put effort into having more positive interactions. Why wouldn't the same be true for your body? You have a relationship with your own body just as much as you do with any other person. The problem is the same; therefore, the solution is the same.

If you have an unhealthy or negative relationship with your body, it's possible that the solution is as simple as having more positive interactions with your body. On the other hand, now is a good time to remind you that this book is not a substitute for seeing a therapist or other professional mentor or guide. If you have a complex body issue, it might be necessary to have someone help you navigate the journey back to a positive relationship with your body. If at any time a practice becomes too much, please stop the practice and consider seeing a professional. Body-based practices are especially difficult for people and there is a higher risk of triggering a trauma reaction or causing distress. You have the responsibility for monitoring yourself during these practices and making decisions that are in your best interest.

3.1

Body Scan

Simplicity is one of the three fundamental principles in Zen philosophy (along with patience and compassion). Laozi wrote in the Tao Te Ching, *'Simple in actions and thoughts, you return to the source of being'* (2). Body scans are a beautiful practice because they are wonderfully simple. It is literally the practice of closing your eyes and directing your full attention systematically to each part of the body in turn. It's a wonderful guided meditation because you can just sit or lie there while someone says each body part and you just bring your attention there, let it rest for a moment, then move on when they say the next one. I highly recommend doing it as a guided meditation either by asking someone to read the practice below or looking one up on YouTube.

Getting into the practice of simplifying has so many benefits – less stress, more confidence, a time saver – take your pick. For some reason, our culture has tricked us into believing that life is complicated. I think that we tell ourselves that life is complicated because it makes us feel better about having a hard time with it. It would be embarrassing if we struggled with something simple. So we say that it is complicated to justify why it's so difficult. Life is not complicated. Our thoughts, expectations, beliefs, and emotions distort reality so that it looks complicated. When we are able to calm the waters and see things as they truly are then we realize that it was actually simple all along. We have stress. We are indecisive because we put so much pressure on ourselves to always make the best choice. The one where no one gets mad. The one where there are no negative consequences. The one that is easiest. The one that other people won't judge. Simplicity is the practice of releasing all of those pressures. It is the practice of trusting yourself. Challenge yourself, if just for today, to let things be simple.

PRACTICE

Body Scan

1. Decide if you want to do this one by yourself or let it be guided.
2. Find a quiet place to lie, sit, or stand and get comfortable.
3. Close your eyes.
4. Bring your attention to each body part in turn, letting it rest there for a moment before moving on to the next.
5. Right big toe.
6. Right second toe.
7. Right third toe.
8. Right fourth toe.
9. Right pinkie toe.
10. Top of the right foot.
11. Bottom of the right foot.
12. Right heel.
13. Right ankle.
14. Right shin.
15. Right calf.
16. Right knee.
17. Right thigh.
18. Right hip.
19. Right buttock.
20. The entire right leg as a unit.
21. Left big toe.
22. Left second toe.
23. Left third toe.
24. Left fourth toe.
25. Left pinkie toe.
26. Top of the left foot.
27. Bottom of the left foot.

28. Left heel.
29. Left ankle.
30. Left shin.
31. Left calf.
32. Left knee.
33. Left thigh.
34. Left hip.
35. Left buttock.
36. The entire left leg as a unit.
37. The entire lower body as a unit.
38. Lower back.
39. Mid back.
40. Upper back.
41. Space between the shoulders.
42. Belly.
43. Ribs.
44. Chest.
45. Right shoulder.
46. Right upper arm.
47. Right elbow.
48. Right forearm.
49. Right wrist.
50. Right palm.
51. Right thumb.
52. Right index finger.
53. Right middle finger.
54. Right ring finger.
55. Right pinkie finger.
56. The whole right arm as a unit.
57. Left shoulder.
58. Left upper arm.
59. Left elbow.
60. Left forearm.
61. Left wrist.

62. Left palm.
63. Left thumb.
64. Left index finger.
65. Left middle finger.
66. Left ring finger.
67. Left pinkie finger.
68. The whole left arm as a unit.
69. Back of the neck.
70. Throat.
71. Jaw.
72. Tongue.
73. Left cheek.
74. Right cheek.
75. Nose.
76. Eyes.
77. Eyebrows.
78. The space between the eyebrows.
79. Forehead.
80. Brain.
81. Top of the head.
82. The entire body as a unit.
83. The whole body together.
84. Allow your mind to rest on the phrase, 'the whole body together' for several moments.
85. Wake your body up slowly by wiggling fingers and toes, maybe taking a big stretch.
86. Blink your eyes open and notice the effects of your practice.

3.2

Progressive Muscle Relaxation

Any good trauma therapist will tell you, the body stores stress. Tension, stress, hurt. We hold it all in our bodies and carry it around every day, usually without even realizing it. Sure, we know our neck, shoulder, knees, and stomach hurt. What we don't know is that it's because we're clenching our muscles all the dang time. Imagine how sore and tired your hands would be if you walked around all day with them clenched into fists? That's basically what your shoulders and jaw are like. This is one of those times that you've got to pay special attention to something because otherwise you'll miss it. I could say, 'with your exhale, release all the tension in your muscles', but your jaw is still clenched because you don't even realize that you're doing it! It's also one of those beautiful times that just paying attention to something helps you fix it. Every time you remember your jaw or your shoulders, you check in with it, and relax.

Baseline is just a fancy word that means normal. If you imagine a scale from 1 to 10 where one is the least stressed and 10 is the most stressed, then your typical rating is your baseline. Take a moment to decide what your typical stress level is (1 is Buddhist monk and 10 is an erupting volcano). Regardless of your baseline, 10 is still the same. 10 is that place where you're angry, irritable, exhausted, hopeless, and just over it all. If you chose a 7, then you're only 3 stressful or irritating events away from snapping at your kids or crying over dropping a pencil (I've been there). Think of meditation as resetting your baseline. You don't have to be used to dealing with it. You don't have to find neck pain normal. You are allowed to exist in a more peaceful and calm state of being.

PRACTICE

Progressive Muscle Relaxation

1. This practice is most beneficial when you're sitting or lying down.
2. Close your eyes and breathe deeply for a few moments.
3. When you're ready, start your practice.
4. Below is a list of muscle groups in order. With your inhale, tense the muscle. With your exhale, release the muscle.
5. Toes (spread as wide as you can).
6. Point toes down (shin/calf).
7. Bring toes to knee (shin/calf).
8. Squeeze thighs together.
9. Buttocks.
10. Arch your back.
11. Take a big breath in, filling your belly, and release to relax all the organs in your abdomen.
12. Bring your shoulder blades together.
13. Make a fist and bring your fists firmly to your shoulders, bending your elbows.
14. Flex fists down.
15. Extend fists up.
16. Bring shoulders to ears. Open mouth wide and stick tongue out.
17. Smile big.
18. Open eyes wide.
19. Breathe normally for a few moments and scan your body.
20. Repeat the practice for any muscle that still feels tense.
21. Allow yourself time to enjoy the effects of your practice.

3.3

Hand Washing

If you thought mindful meditation is just about doing new stuff, then you are partly correct. A lot of times, mindfulness is about doing the same stuff you already do, but in a new way. You already breathe, now you breathe mindfully. You are present with your in breath. You are present with your out breath. You already have a body. Now you are present with every part of your body. You already wash your hands. Now you wash your hands mindfully. You are aware of the sound of the water, the temperature of the water, the feel of the water running through your hands. You notice the way you move your hands effortlessly – without even thinking – to turn the water on, to get soap, to rub together in a habitual way, then to get a towel and dry them. You notice the smell of the soap and your immediate reaction to it, whether attraction (yes, please, give me more!) or aversion (ew! Gross, no thank you!). Essentially, you already live, but now you are present in your life.

Washing your hands is an everyday – or several times a day – occurrence. Is it possible that it could be exciting and there could be something new to notice every time? They say that no man ever steps in the same river twice because he is not the same man and the river, constantly moving, is not the same river. Could you let this be true of every experience in every moment? Could you believe that every moment of your life is worth being present for? Perhaps you are telling yourself that you don't have time to slow down and notice the seemingly meaningless parts of your life. The raindrops chasing each other down the window. The clouds in the sky. Brushing your teeth. What if it is these small moments that make up a life more than any 'big' thing?

PRACTICE

Mindful Hand Washing

1. Wash your hands.
2. Watch as your body naturally completes the task in a routine and memorized pattern.
3. Notice the water, the soap, and the feeling of your hands rubbing together.
4. Be present for this chance to connect with your hands.
5. Take a moment when you're finished to close your eyes and notice the effects of your practice.

3.4

Neck Rolls

I love neck rolls because they just feel so good. If you're like most people, then you probably carry a lot of stress in your neck and shoulders which means they're tight and uncomfortable a lot of the time. This is actually a major cause of chronic headaches and migraines, as are dehydration and tiredness. Drinking water and getting enough sleep are acts of self-care. Think of this practice like a conversation between your awareness and your neck. You're saying, "Hey neck, how are you feeling today? What do you need from me?" then listening as your neck gives you the answer. You might choose to stay in one place and breathe for a few rounds, or you might choose to just keep it moving because the flow feels amazing. You might choose to go deeper and really get into those deep muscles. You might choose to keep it shallow with only a slight movement here or there. The key is, you're in tune with your body and respecting the messages that you're receiving.

If you're reading this and you've already decided what your movement is going to look like and how far you're going to push yourself, stop. Breathe in and out three times. And re-read this passage with fresh eyes. Planning out what to do before even starting the practice is assuming you already know what your body wants. It's moving with your mind. The practice is for the mind to listen and respect the body. No planning. No forcing. The body gets the control. The whole time. So often our mind fills in ahead of time what we *think* is going to happen, what someone is going to say, or how we're going to feel, so we stop paying attention to what is *actually* happening. Rehearsing conversations, cutting people off in the middle of a sentence, getting anxious about a future event. It's all projections based on what your mind expects. Paying attention moment to moment gives your life the opportunity to be different. Even better, it gives you the opportunity to respond to your life in the reality of what is.

PRACTICE

Neck Rolls

1. Sit comfortably with your back straight and your shoulders relaxed.
2. Breathe in and out several times feeling grounded (exhale) through your tailbone and lifted through the crown of your head (inhale).
3. Exhale lower your head so your chin meets your chest.
4. Stay here for a full cycle of breath noticing any sensations.
5. Inhale and return your head to center.
6. Exhale left ear to left shoulder; stay for a cycle or two of breaths.
7. Inhale and return to center.
8. Exhale right ear to right shoulder; stay for a cycle or two of breaths.
9. Inhale to center.
10. Exhale chin to chest; stay here or ride the exhale as you roll right ear to right shoulder.
11. Inhale and stay or roll gently back with face toward sky then left ear to left shoulder.
12. The exhale carries you from left ear/left shoulder, down through chin to chest, and around to right ear/right shoulder.
13. The inhale completes the circle back and around.
14. Complete three cycles, then at the bottom of an exhale switch and complete three cycles in the opposite direction.
15. Return your head to center and breathe. Notice the effects of your practice.

3.5

Underappreciated Body Part

It can be really easy to forget we have a body. It's just 'me'. Or is it? Bodies are more like factories. It's a system of workers and departments all with jobs to do so that the whole body functions properly. Your toe is just you, right? It's actually skin, muscle, bone, blood, fat, arteries, veins, capillaries, neurons, and so much more, all made up of cells and minerals. Cells are the workers at the factory and there are so many different jobs. Blood cells, skin cells, nerve cells, bone cells, muscle cells, fat cells, and more. They transport nutrients, bile, and water. They hold you upright and help you move. They transmit information from every part of your body to your brain for processing and then carry the messages wherever they need to go. They do all the jobs that your body needs in order to live, grow, and reproduce. You might think that your brain controls all this, but actually, every cell already has all the information that it needs to do its job. Your brain is even made up of cells! Your brain is essentially cells, fat, water, blood, and soft tissue. Though they have some ideas, scientists still don't truly understand how brain activity translates into thoughts, dreams, creativity, and imagination.

Think about all the things your body does every day. Your eyes see. Your ears hear. Your brain processes. Your lungs pump air. Your heart pumps blood. You have a whole bunch of organs to digest food. Your feet carry you around. Your butt lets you sit comfortably. You have hands to touch, grab, type, and do a whole variety of things! It's amazing what your body does every day; yet so often we are not mindful, we do not remember that we have hardworking bodies. We think bad things about our body. We might even hate our body for this reason or that reason. Can you let yourself rest in the comfort that your body is doing its best to take care of you? Are you willing to spend some time remembering and practicing gratitude for your body? Take some time now to reflect on a body part that you feel is particularly underappreciated. This body part works hard for you and makes your life better. This body part is an important part of your ability to live and enjoy life. Got one?

Underappreciated Body Part

1. Sit, stand, or lay in a quiet and comfortable place.
2. Set your timer for three minutes.
3. Close your eyes.
4. Breathe in and out several times to prepare your body and mind for meditation.
5. Shine the light of your awareness on the body part of your choice.
6. Let yourself be filled with gratitude, maybe even sending some words of thankfulness to that place.
7. Continue to breathe and focus on this place until your timer sounds.
8. Release the attention on the body part and give yourself time to notice the effects of this practice.

3.6

Loving Touch

Gary Chapman wrote a book designed for married couples, called *The Five Love Languages,* which explains five different ways to express and receive love. He said that love is recognized in types of actions and people see and share love differently, which can sometimes cause problems if there is a disconnect in the relationship. The five love languages from his book are acts of service, words of affirmation, physical touch, quality time, and gifts. Suppose that a person values and understands quality time as love, but their partner speaks love as gifts. The partner may give this person jewelry, trinkets, clothes, or other things, expecting that their partner will feel loved. But they don't. They become hurt and resentful. How confusing for the partner! The important takeaways from the book are several fold. It's important to be self-aware so that you can communicate to others how you want to be loved. You may have to change the way you show others love so that they are able to understand it and feel loved. It would be helpful if you can learn to feel loved when someone expresses love in a way that is not your primary language. This type of awareness, mental flexibility, and clarity is mindfulness. Here's the kicker, you can apply the same principles to your relationship with yourself!

I'm going to provide some examples from each love language to give you ideas about how you might show yourself love in a variety of ways. Feel free to add your own, explore anything further, or even go online to take a quiz about your love language. These are in no particular order. Physical touch is pretty self-explanatory. It applies if you feel loved by someone actually touching you – holding your hand, rubbing your shoulders, brushing their hand along you as they walk by, getting hugs, and so forth. You could show love to yourself in this way by doing a self-massage, being mindful when you apply lotion, scheduling yourself for a massage, or just engaging in any kind of positive skin to skin contact with yourself. Words of affirmation is your primary language if you feel most loved when someone compliments or verbally appreciates you, writes you notes, or in any other way uses words in a positive way with you. You may also be especially hurt by any kind of unloving speech. You can show yourself love in this way by practicing daily affirmations, having a regular gratitude practice, working on increasing positive thoughts, and boosting your overall positive self-talk. Quality time directly relates to feeling loved when someone is truly present with you – playing games, doing activities together, watching movies, etc. You can show yourself love in this way by prioritizing time for hobbies, setting aside a few minutes to connect with yourself, or in any other way giving yourself the gift of quality time. Note that it may be especially hurtful when you (or others) are not present, either on the phone or otherwise distracted during time together.

The language of gifts is about receiving things. Some people judge themselves for having gifts as their love language because they think it makes them shallow. I personally love receiving gifts, but my favorite part about it is seeing what other people pick out for me. I feel loved knowing they saw something, thought of me, and purchased it to bring me happiness. You can practice this language in isolation or in combination with another language. Consider buying yourself a new lotion or bubble bath, a new movie, game, or crafting supply. The fifth and final language is acts of service. Traditionally, acts of service could be things like cooking a meal, cleaning, helping with a task, or otherwise physically doing something to make the other person's life easier. When you get enough sleep, drink water, eat healthy food, exercise, or otherwise support your body to function well then you are practicing acts of service with yourself.

PRACTICE

Hand Massage
(A physical touch practice for self-love)

1. Find a comfortable, calm space to sit.
2. Breathe in and out three times to prepare yourself for meditation.
3. Gently hold your left hand in your right so that your four fingers are on the back of your hand and your thumb is on the palm.
4. Starting near the wrist, use firm pressure while moving your thumb from wrist to base of each finger.
5. If it feels particularly good, do it a second time.
6. Next, wrap your right hand around each finger in turn and use a twisting motion with medium pressure to massage out from base to tip.
7. Repeat the same process to massage the right hand.
8. Sit with your eyes closed for several moments to observe the effects of this practice.

3.7

Hear Your Heartbeat

Heartbeats are such a wonderful and gentle reminder that we are alive. A miraculous bump, bump, bump calling us to be present. Hearts are definitely one of those things that you don't notice until it's causing you problems, whether it's just discomfort from exercise, a scary or stressful situation, or maybe even a heart attack. You may also recall that the heart is part of that system of automatic functions that respond when your brain sounds the red alert 'stressful situation' alarm. Your heart gets the message that your body needs to respond to a threat, so it jumps in to pump faster and harder so that your blood can carry messengers, nutrients, and warmth to the necessary places. Sometimes this is helpful, and we appreciate it, as when we're exercising. Sometimes, like during a panic attack, it makes us feel like we're dying. Your heart is a good measure of how your body is doing. Slow, steady, soft heartbeat? Relaxed body. Fast, hard, chaotic heartbeat? Stressed, sick, or overworked body.

Luckily for us, our breath and our heart are friends. What I mean by that is, you don't have control over your heart rate, but you do have control over your breath and your breath is part of the system that tells the heart how to beat. By slowing down, smoothing out, and deepening our breath, our heart gets the message that it should also be in a state of relaxed calm. They've actually done studies that show that what you think about affects your heart rate. Scientists prompted people to think about sad, stressful, scary, or irritating things and their heart rate increased. Then people were asked to think about calming, comforting, and peaceful things and their heart rates decreased. It's pretty amazing how fast it happens too – less than a minute! Your body listens to your thoughts. If you're

71

thinking things like, "I can't take any more", "this is too much", "there's no way out", or "he doesn't love me anymore", then your body hears that and responds by going into stress mode. They say that stress is an internal reaction to an external event because it has more to do with the way that you're thinking about a situation than about the situation itself. Think about it, two people in the same situation – one person gets stressed, and the other person doesn't. Clearly, it's not about the situation. It's about the way you're thinking about it.

PRACTICE

Hear Your Heartbeat

1. Find a quiet, peaceful place and get comfortable.
2. Set your timer for three minutes.
3. Close your eyes.
4. Breathe in and out a few times to prepare yourself for meditation.
5. Find your heartbeat – hear it in your ears, feel it in your chest, throat, or wrist, or tune into its rhythm somewhere else in your body.
6. This might take time, and that's okay.
7. Once you find it, just listen.
8. Let yourself be comforted by its steady chug.
9. Once your timer sounds, leave your eyes closed a moment to notice the effects of your practice.

Week 4

Working with Emotions

Life is simple. Society has passed down the lie that life is complicated, perhaps as a way to help us feel better about having a hard time. Think about it, if we had a hard time with something simple then we would feel stupid or incompetent, but it's only natural to have a hard time with something complicated, right? What if, this whole time, it wasn't life that's complicated but something else. Consider that life is really simple, but it's our emotions that make it seem complicated. More accurately, it's our relationship with our emotions that makes life appear complicated. There are a couple of misperceptions (incorrect ways of seeing things) that we're working with here. One is the wrong belief that life is complicated. Second is the wrong belief that emotions are the problem and therefore getting rid of them is the solution. Remember from our work with alternate nostril breathing that nothing is wrong. There is nothing to get rid of. There are only things which are imbalanced and misunderstood which cause disharmony. The solution is therefore to understand and to balance.

It may not surprise you to learn that you work with emotions the same way that you work with anything else: by giving yourself the opportunity to have a calm encounter with them, anchored by mindful breathing. Thich Nhat Hanh said that meditation is the practice of looking deeply into the nature of things. Jon Kabat-Zinn calls meditation a serene encounter with reality. I have come to learn that the first step to managing anything is to keep calm and be kind. Did you ever play hot and cold as a child? It's a game where someone hides something, and another person tries to find it. The person gives clues 'you're getting hotter' to indicate they're getting closer to the item, or 'you're colder than ice!' to say they're very far from the item. This is like emotions except that emotions are sometimes based on wrong information.

Our brain is pretty cool in that it uses a lot of different types of information to determine our emotional reaction at any given moment. Emotions are based on present-moment experiences, your physical state (sick, tired, hungry – oof, right?), memories, previous experiences, expectations, goals, and don't even get me started on hormones! Our brain creates a story for us so that our world makes sense. Unfortunately, the brain makes mistakes. Sometimes the story that it creates for us is not accurate. An important step in creating balance and harmony in your emotions is realizing that you are not your emotions. Emotions are your body's messengers to you and they're not always telling you an accurate story. A meditation practice gives you the opportunity to look deeply and peacefully into the true essence, the foundation, of your emotions. I guarantee there are stories there that you haven't even let yourself hear yet. It can be a bumpy ride, but until the messengers are heard, they do not leave.

4.1

Clouds in the Sky

Clouds are really wonderful. There is a complete cycle between bodies of water on the earth to hanging water clumps in the sky so that nothing is lost, and everything is gained. Clouds provide shade and enjoyment. Rain helps the plants grow. Bodies of water provide life, vegetation, transportation, and all sorts of things. I think the most wonderful thing about clouds is that they come in all shapes and sizes. Sometimes you look up at a blue sky sprinkled with misty white clouds. Other times you look up and it's like the blue sky is gone and there's a blanket of thick, dark gray in its place. Countless hours have been spent by people all over the world looking up at clouds and using creativity and imagination to come up with stories and creatures. What a wonderful world.

Clouds are also a helpful metaphor for emotions. Clouds come and go. Whether you want them to or not, whether you even notice them or not. Sometimes clouds are pleasant and bring you a moment of happiness. Other times you might blame the cloud for your suffering. Still the cloud comes and goes. Sometimes it might seem like all there is, is dark gray clouds and the blue sky will never come back. Still, behind the clouds, the blue sky is always there. Sometimes the clouds come with thunder, lightning, and heavy rains. You might be able to go inside and get cozy and dry. You might have to sit outside in the cold rain. Sometimes you could go inside and be cozy, but for whatever reason you sit outside in the cold rain anyway. So often we cling to our clouds and say, 'This is *my* cloud'. We chase it. What might life be like if we could sit peacefully and watch the clouds go by, appreciating each for its momentary presence in our life. Not feeling the need to do anything. Just sitting. Just breathing.

PRACTICE

Watching the Clouds

1. There are two ways to do this: meditate somewhere that you can actually watch the sky or close your eyes and complete this practice as a visualization.
2. Find your meditation place and get comfortable.
3. Set your timer for three or five minutes.
4. Breathe in and out several times to prepare for meditation.
5. If you are watching the sky, simply watch it until your timer sounds. Tuning in to the movement of the clouds if there are any.
6. If you're doing this practice as a visualization, then close your eyes.
7. Call to mind an image of a sky.
8. See yourself, the observer, looking up at the sky watching the clouds go by.
9. Feel what there is to feel. See what there is to see.
10. Once your timer sounds, release the visualization.
11. Notice the effects of your practice.

4.2

Wounded Child

Remember when you were a child and you got hurt. You would run to someone crying and upset and they would reach out to comfort you. You might not. You may not have had a person who was there to comfort you. Either way, we all have a wounded child in us. A child who was hurt, betrayed, embarrassed, insecure, mistreated, neglected, made fun of, or left alone. The Buddhists believe that the wounded child is passed from generation to generation, handing down suffering from parent to child. The practice is the same whether you believe that you are transforming the suffering from your own life or from the lives of generations before you. That wounded child is inside you and continues to show itself as anger, sadness, judgment, anxiety, mistrust, despair, resentment, and apathy. Your wounded child needs to be seen, heard, understood, and comforted. You need to be healed.

Imagine you break your ankle. You could decide not to go to a doctor and just continue on with your life as if it's not broken. It's still broken. It's swollen. It's painful. You're causing more damage to it by pretending it's fine than by acknowledging that it's not and getting help. Despite what you might believe, pretending that something is fine does not make it fine. Pretending that your childhood doesn't affect you, doesn't keep it from affecting you. In order to heal you have to recognize that you're hurting. You have to rest. When you rest your body has an amazing ability to heal itself. When you rest you free up resources inside you that your body uses to go to work fixing whatever is damaged. Mindful meditation provides the opportunity for a calm mind and body. In his book, *The Heart of the Buddha's Teaching: Transforming Suffering into Peace, Joy, and*

Liberation, Thich Nhat Hanh once said, *"Calming allows us to rest, and resting is a precondition for healing"* (3). I'm not saying you hack away at your inner child on some kind of ferocious quest to get rid of it. In fact, I'm saying just the opposite. You spend time with your inner child in kindness and understanding so that you are both comforted and healed.

PRACTICE

Talking to Your Wounded Child

1. Find a peaceful, comfortable place for your practice; I recommend sitting, but use your own intuition.
2. Take several breaths in and out to release all expectations for this practice.
3. See a version of your younger self approach you.
4. Continue to be anchored by your breath.
5. Listen to whatever they have to say.
6. Your only job is to breathe in a way that offers peace and calming.
7. If you feel yourself getting sucked in to an old emotion, breathe.
8. Feel yourself sitting in this moment.
9. When your practice feels complete, place your hands over your heart for a while and notice the effects of your practice.

***Buddhists recommend doing this practice daily for 5-10 minutes. Healing takes time.

4.3

Anger Mantra

Buddhist psychology teaches that the brain is a garden with many types of seeds. Seeds for anger, resentment, judgment, violence, prejudice, and so forth. Seeds for kindness, compassion, love, understanding, creativity, and peace. The seeds that flourish and grow to show themselves in our lives are the seeds that are cultivated, much like in a regular garden. Imagine planting one seed in a corner of the field that gets no water, no sunlight, and the soil is rocky and nutrientless. The farmer does not care for the seed or nurture it. The seed is not going to grow. It's not going to manifest (become real) in any meaningful way. Meanwhile, there is a seed that is planted in good soil, has sunlight, water, and the farmer cares for it diligently. That seed, naturally, thrives and grows big and strong.

Similarly, there is a traditional Native American story about a Cherokee brave and his grandson. One day the grandfather tells his grandson about a battle inside each of us between two wolves. One wolf is evil – filled with anger, hatred, jealousy, guilt, self-pity, greed, and arrogance. The other wolf is good – filled with love, joy, peace, patience, kindness, generosity, empathy, compassion, and faith. The young grandson thinks for a moment then asks his grandfather, "which one wins?" and the Cherokee brave replies simply, "The one you feed".

These stories – from opposite sides of the earth – tell us that our emotional reactions are as much a product of past as they are of present. Our history of behaving, thinking, and responding influences the strength of the current emotion. It takes time and awareness to change those habitual patterns of responding. The Buddhist version also recognizes influences outside of ourselves. The environment can water seeds of anger or of kindness. If you associate only with people who are angry and critical, they are watering seeds of judgment, doubt, and insecurity in you. Mindfulness gives you the opportunity to either move your plant out of their rain or put up a shield so you don't get wet.

PRACTICE

Thich Nhat Hanh's Anger Mantra

1. This can be practiced either of two ways: sit in a peaceful place and call to mind a memory which evokes anger (or simply allow yourself to feel angry) or use this in a moment where you are currently experiencing anger.
2. Breathing in, I know that anger is here.
3. Breathing out, I know that anger is not me.
4. Breathing in, I know that anger is unpleasant.
5. Breathing out, I know this feeling will pass.
6. Breathing in, I am calm.
7. Breathing out, I am strong enough to take care of this anger.
8. Repeat the mantra 3-5 times or until you feel calm.
9. Breathe freely for a few moments and notice the effects of your practice.

4.4

Kindness Journaling

It's time to look deeply into the meaning of kindness. At its core, I truly believe that kindness is about being present with someone. When you remember that you exist, and the other person exists then you can appreciate the moment that you're sharing and their impact on your life. A word or action which relieves another person's suffering or brings them a moment of happiness – that is kindness. A sincere acknowledgement of how another person's existence improves your own – that is kindness. If you Google search 'kindness' you will find that it is both an act and a quality – being friendly, generous, and considerate. There are three parts here. First, you remember that the other person exists. Second, you offer a gift in word, act, or material item without any expectation of personal gain. Third, you interact in a way that is non-harming and pleasant for the person. The goal of kindness is to create an environment where people feel seen, accepted, and appreciated. We all want to feel like valuable human beings. What a wonderful gift to be able to offer to someone.

Because life is about balance, it's time to talk about what kindness is *not*. Kindness is not letting yourself be mistreated. Kindness is not overcommitting yourself. Kindness is not empty flattery. Kindness is not a tool to get people to like you or do things for you. Kindness is not neglecting yourself to do things for others. Pema Chodron does a lot of teaching on kindness and compassion. The essence being that kindness has to start with you. Kindness to yourself is step one. Then, when you are filled with kindness, it will naturally pour out of you to reach other people. One of my parents' frequently quoted Bible teachings is, *"Out of the overflow of the heart, the mouth speaks"* (Matthew 12:34 [4]). Essentially, whatever you spend time cultivating on the inside becomes obvious on the outside. The more you redirect your thoughts to kindness, understanding, and empathy, then the more these things will show in your words and your actions.

PRACTICE

Kindness Journaling

1. Get paper and pen and go to your quiet, comfortable space.
2. Close your eyes and breathe in and out several times to prepare yourself for your meditation.
3. Set your timer for five or seven minutes.
4. Reflect on an act of kindness that meant a lot to you.
5. Write about how this made you feel and why it was so meaningful.
6. You can write this as a journal entry or a letter to the kind person.
7. If you finish before your timer sounds allow yourself to re-read your words or simply to reflect on the feelings or action.
8. Once your timer sounds, close your eyes again and notice the effects of your practice.
9. If you wrote a letter, decide whether or not you want to send it.

4.5

Mantra Meditations

There's a lot of misunderstanding about what a mantra is and how it's used. If you're a person who hears the word 'mantra' and automatically you shut down, then this is for you. Mantras are not magic. Mantras are not spells. There is nothing special about saying any particular word. The word mantra is Sanskrit for sacred message or counsel. The purpose of a mantra is to improve concentration and focus during a meditation. There's an old story about a small village in India. Every year they had a parade to celebrate the end of monsoon season. The most honored guest was the village elephant. They were so proud to have an elephant and loved to display him during the parade. The problem was, every year the elephant would wreak havoc by flailing his trunk around, grabbing bananas, knocking the roof off carts, toppling things over. It was a mess. One year, the elephant handler gave the elephant a bamboo stick to hold. The elephant marched proudly with his baton held high. His trunk never once wavered, and it was the most joyous parade the village had ever had. Your mantra is like a stick of bamboo for your unruly mind.

In various traditions mantras are handed down from teacher to student. In some practices, you are instructed to keep your mantra secret. For those who follow those beliefs, then they would disagree with my earlier statements about the lack of inherent power in a mantra. Let's focus instead on the use of a mantra to deepen your meditation practice. Your mantra could be the same every time you meditate, or you could choose to select a different mantra based on the purpose of your meditation. For example, a lot of people choose to use the name of their higher power as their mantra. They sit in silent meditation and chant inwardly, 'Jesus, Jesus, Jesus', 'Hare Krishna, Hare Krishna, Hare Krishna', 'Allah, Allah, Allah' as a way to bring their higher power closer to them by increasing deep awareness. Some people also use qualities that they want to cultivate such as kindness, understanding, love, compassion, joy, or calm. Mantras could be one word, a phrase, or a series of phrases. Often mantras are linked to a breath practice, but this is not necessary. Some argue that by linking the mantra to the breath then you disrupt the natural ability for the breath to meet the needs of the body. I say, try out a bunch of different stuff and see what works for you. It's best to choose one for a practice and stick with it, though, jumping around from mantra to mantra is kind of chaotic for a meditation practice.

PRACTICE

Using a Mantra

1. Find a comfortable and peaceful place to sit, stand, or lie down.
2. Decide on your mantra. If you're having trouble settling on one, maybe try 'I am here'.
3. Set your timer for three, five, or seven minutes.
4. Close your eyes and breathe in and out three times before beginning to recite your mantra silently (you could say it out loud if you're feeling it).
5. One your timer sounds, sit in silence for several moments to feel the effects of your practice.

4.6

Existing in a Frustrating Situation

You may recall from the beginning of this book that I pointed out that it is not the purpose of meditation to get better at meditating. Meditation is a practice to retrain your brain how to pay attention, respond to various situations, and to nurture seeds of kindness, generosity, compassion, creativity, and peace within us. They say you don't get to practice life. That is partly correct. In a sense, meditation is practice for life. The benefits of a meditation practice are not wholly experienced on the mat, although it is enjoyable to meditate. The benefits of meditation are seen when we leave the meditation space and go out to live our lives. You never leave a practice as the same person you were when you began. You are changed. You have transformed yourself by rededicating yourself to your personal values.

All of the practices up until now have started with an instruction to practice in a place that is calm, comfortable, and peaceful. Not anymore. The training wheels are coming off. However, keep in mind that not all frustrating situations are created equal. Imagine a scale of 1 to 10 with 1 being the most peaceful and easy place to meditate and 10 is the most distracting, obnoxious, difficult situation. It's not realistic to practice in level 1 situations and then think you're going to be this peaceful, open-minded saint in a heated conflict or at the Christmas dinner table. You're going to slip back into old patterns. You're going to do and say things you'll regret. It just happens. Your practice is just to keep practicing. As a heads up, you're going to get frustrated. That's the point. Notice any stories that come up in your head, probably disguised as one of two things: you're doing something wrong and/or you're not doing enough. You might find yourself getting frustrated and upset because 'this isn't what meditation is supposed to feel like' or 'I must be doing something wrong'. These are lies and they only make you more frustrated. Just breathe. You're doing everything exactly right. You're learning.

PRACTICE

Meditating with Distractions

1. Find a place with some distractions or irritations (aim for like a two or three on the scale).
2. Set your timer for three or five minutes.
3. Close your eyes.
4. Observe your breath.
5. Maintain a slow, steady, deep breath.
6. Every distraction is a wave on the surface of your awareness.
7. Use your mindful breathing as your anchor.
8. When your timer sounds, give yourself a moment to notice the effects of your practice.

It's normal to get irritated, that's the point. You're helping your brain learn to respond to annoying situations in a different way

4.7

Reflection Journaling

Welcome to the last day of the fourth week. Halfway. It's easy to move from day to day and feel like you're the same person doing the same things as always. Sometimes things happen so slowly that we don't notice – like the frog who accidentally boiled himself in a pot of water over the fire. Every day has challenges so it can feel like we're not accomplishing anything. That's really discouraging. You put in all this time and effort doing the practices – you want to see some results! It's good to get in the habit of setting aside some time every now and then to think back on who you were a month ago, a year ago, ten years ago. Just to see what you see. Your emotions will have a reaction – usually pride, remorse, or a combination of the two. Challenge yourself to practice nonjudgmental awareness. I can see something for what it is without needing to form an opinion about it. There's actually a saying, 'going further and feeling worse' because the more you practice, the deeper you go, and those are the things you've been avoiding for a really long time. Just know that this is a normal part of the process. Don't forget to enjoy yourself along the way.

I read a book by Chris Prentiss called *Zen and the Art of Happiness* and there's a pretty blunt statement at the beginning where he basically says, if you're unhappy then you need to do something different. The point is that your life at this moment is the result of all the choices that you've made in the past. If you like your life now then you're on the right track and you just need to keep doing what you're doing, but if you're unhappy then that's a good indicator that you should try something different. It's not a judgment statement or criticism. It's just an observation. Your choices are not satisfying to you so it's a good idea to make different choices. Having a regular reflection practice helps to bring consistent attention to your path. Are you facing the direction that you want to go, or is it time for a redirect? Every day of your life you have the opportunity to do something different. Remember, change happens in the now. Reflection is not about boosting your ego or being self-critical. It's a practice of honest and nonjudgmental observations of your own nature.

PRACTICE

Reflection Journaling

1. Find a space for your meditation practice. Have a pen and paper.
2. Set your timer for five minutes.
3. Close your eyes and breathe in and out three times to prepare yourself for meditation.
4. Finish this sentence, 'Over the last four weeks, I've become aware that I...'
5. Don't think too hard. Just let the words flow.
6. Remember the goal here is observation. Avoid judgment statements about whether something is 'good' or 'bad'.
7. If you finish writing before your timer sounds, then just sit quietly and breathe. Perhaps re-read what you've written.
8. Once your timer sounds, close your eyes again and allow yourself to notice the effects of your practice.

Week 5

Traditional Mini-Meditations

Lessons are handed down from generation to generation because they matter. There are some meditation techniques that people have used and taught for thousands of years. Because they work. So far, we have practiced being fully present, tuning in with breath, connecting with our bodies, and working with emotions. Now that you've got a feel for what meditation is like, it seems like a good time to introduce some tried and true practices handed down by meditation teachers all over the world. Practicing meditation is not just about improving your own life. It's so much more than that. It is about connecting with yourself, sure, but even more so it's about being a part of something so much bigger than you or me. Meditation is a beautiful tradition connecting every person who practices. I meditate as a result of the practices of all those who have come before me.

The first meditator passed their knowledge on to their students. Those students continued practicing and passed on their teacher's knowledge along with their own new understanding to even more students. And so on and so forth until my own teachers passed it on to me. When I meditate, I connect with the traditions of Buddhism, Christianity, Tao, Zen, Hinduism, Yoga, and so many more. It's a powerful connection that creates shared humanity across time and space. Your practice is not just for you. It honors those who came before you and cultivates the seeds in you for you to water those same seeds in everyone you meet. You are a part of something big. You are a wave. When you meditate, you become part of the whole ocean.

In Buddhism, there is a belief that there is a Buddha in every person. The Buddha inside represents the place that is purely kind and loving. The practice of bringing your hands together and bowing is recognition of the Buddha nature that lives in the other person. There is a popular Buddhist blessing that can be used (I sometimes say it internally, so I don't make people uncomfortable since they probably won't understand), 'A flower for you, a Buddha to be'. Similarly, yoga practices often end with Namaste which is a recognition of the same energy living in every person. Namaste is often translated as, "I honor the place in you which is the same in me". Whether you truly believe that every person shares an energy or internal connection, I think we can all agree that we all have some shared experiences just for the simple reason that we're all human. We all suffer. We all want to be loved. We all eat, breathe, and poop. I choose to believe that we're all doing the best we can with the information we have. Either way, these traditional meditation practices have been passed down, shared across time and space, and have landed themselves in this book in front of your eyes. As you practice, remember that every time you meditate you are a part of something bigger than yourself.

5.1

Candle Meditation

Modern life is full of distractions – calls, texts, social media, seemingly endless notifications, TV, political drama, world catastrophes, thoughts, feelings. It's so easy to become unfocused. Like a rabbit darting off in this direction then that direction, distractions have us running around and exhausting ourselves without actually accomplishing anything. We are pulled in so many directions because so many things are important to us and that's a beautiful thing. We care about work, hobbies, relationships, ourselves. We care about avoiding things that are unpleasant, fixing problems, and getting more of the things that bring us joy. There are those who say that everything in life causes a reaction of either attraction or aversion, and if we are not aware of this then we become slaves to our preferences.

Focus is the ability to stay in line with our goals regardless of distractions. Focus means that the goal is the most important thing and everything else falls away. Imagine you are a piece of metal moving along a path. On either side are magnets, some with the positive side towards you and some with the negative. It's easy to waver. It's natural (literally) to waver. That's what metal does, it moves toward or away from magnets. Mindful meditation brings compassionate awareness to this process and gives you the power to consistently move toward your goal. Do you sway side to side? Of course, that's a force of nature. And you always move forward. Always toward your goal. A moth to a flame.

PRACTICE

Candle Meditation

1. Find a dark place – the darkest place I've found is the bathroom with the lights off.
2. Light a candle and put it directly in front of you – it's best if you can watch the flame flicker, so maybe not one in a glass jar.
3. Set your timer for seven or ten minutes.
4. Close your eyes and breathe in and out three times to prepare for your practice.
5. Open your eyes. Look directly at the flame.
6. Let your eyes relax, going unfocused. Blinking as little as is comfortable for you.
7. If at any time your mind wanders, bring your full attention back to the flame.
8. Once your timer sounds, close your eyes and breathe for a while noticing the effects of your meditation.

5.2

Walking Meditation

There is a beautiful poem by Thich Nhat Hanh simply titled, *"Walking Meditation"*. Thinking of walking as a meditation highlights the ability to tap into every act of every day as a way to connect deeply and unceasingly. Every time your foot connects with the earth is a call back to the present moment. Step. Step. Step. Connect. Connect. Connect. Every muscle in your body working together to move you toward your goal. Perhaps one of the most challenging lessons to learn is that you do not need to find anything. Love, peace, happiness. There is no search. It is always there all around you. Your task is not to find it, but to let yourself experience it. Happiness is here. Can you feel it? Peace is in every moment. What walls need to come down in your heart and mind to let you feel the wonderful miracle of life?

Take your shoes off. Take your socks off. Let your feet connect with the floor. Walk on the grass. Walk on the sidewalk. Give yourself the opportunity to feel whatever is beneath you. There are textures and experiences that are just waiting for you to notice them. When you walk, know that you are walking in the same way as Queen Elizabeth walked, as George Washington walked, as any human ever born has ever walked. When you are walking there is so much to notice – the movement of your body, the sensations on your foot, your posture, the sights and sounds all around you. Drink them all in. Enjoy your walk.

Walking Meditation

Walk – I recommend barefoot.

5.3

Loving Kindness (Metta)

Some lessons we have to learn over and over again. There's a difference between learning a skill (multiplication tables, driving a car, reading) and retraining the way that you think about and respond to situations. You only have to learn math once. You don't know how to add or subtract fractions? It looks hard and overwhelming. Someone teaches you how to add and subtract fractions. You practice for a while. It's easy and you add and subtract fractions like a pro. That's a skill. You make a mistake, and your immediate thought is, 'why are you so dumb?'. You catch yourself, breathe in and out, and reframe the thought, 'I made a mistake. Mistakes happen. I'll try to pay better attention next time'.You learned how to be kind to yourself, right? You are partly correct.

The next time you make a mistake you'll probably still find yourself saying, 'why are you so dumb?', but every time you catch yourself and reframe to a kinder thought you are creating the habit of thinking kindly. Every time someone cuts you off in traffic and you gently remind yourself that it's not helpful or worth it to get upset, or even that your anger is coming from a place of fear (reckless driving puts your life at risk and triggers that fight/flight stress response) then you're creating the habit of remaining calm in that situation. Anytime you notice a reaction and softly redirect to a preferred way of responding then you are creating the habit of responding in that way. Some reactions live deeper inside us than others and are harder to root out. You might take things personally, make assumptions, or have strict rules about the way that people should behave. These things require consistent redirection and reminders to yourself that you are creating new habits.

PRACTICE

Loving Kindness Meditation

1. Find a place to meditate. Sit, stand, or lie down.
2. Close your hands and breathe in and out three times to prepare for your practice.
3. Consider bringing your hands together in front of your heart if that feels right to you.
4. Say these words to yourself: May I be happy. May I be healthy. May I be at peace.
5. Breathe for a few moments and let these messages reverberate inside you.
6. Call to mind the image of a loved one (or perhaps someone that you're struggling with).
7. Say these words to yourself: May you be happy. May you be healthy. May you be at peace.
8. Breathe in and out several times, allowing the words more space than just the time it takes to say them.
9. Let yourself become aware of every living person or every living creature.
10. May you be happy. May you be healthy. May you be at peace.
11. Breathe and allow your loving kindness to radiate from you to every living creature.
12. Release the practice. Notice the effects of your meditation.

5.4

Mountain Pose Meditation

Mountain pose, or tadasana, is a yoga pose that a lot of people misinterpret as just standing. There are physical guides for correct posture, alignment, and weight positioning which use your body's bone structure and muscles to stand in the most supported way. There are also energetic cues to create an experience of being firmly grounded and stable while also feeling lifted and tall. Mountain pose is about taking up space. Being as big and firm as you can be. Standing resolutely in your truth. Mountain pose is a call to embody (become the physical form of) all the properties of a mountain. Recall that the word 'yoga' means connection. When you think of a mountain, what aspects of a mountain can you connect with? Some words that come to my mind are: firm, solid, stable, immovable, resolute, undaunted, formidable, intimidating, or regal. As you stand in mountain pose, let yourself connect with these parts of your own mountain.

I'm going to walk you through some of the body positioning and energetic cues for a traditional mountain pose. This is a standing posture. Start with your feet – place them about shoulder width apart with toes and knees facing forward (the insides of your feet might make a little upside-down V with your toes slightly closer together than your heels). Lift up all ten of your toes and then carefully put them down one at a time. Rock forward and backward, side to side. Feel the weight shift – get curious, see how far you can go in each direction without falling. Find the place where everything feels balanced. This is your foundation. Take the time to feel steady because everything builds from here. Feel your shins stacked over your ankles. Your knees slightly bent, not locked straight (perhaps the term 'micro-bend' is helpful). Feel your thighs drawing together. Unclench your butt (maybe do an inhale – clench, exhale – unclench situation). Imagine your pelvis like a bowl of water. You can tilt your hips side to side, backward and forward, just like with your feet. Play with the movement a little bit, then find that place where it is level, so no water spills out. Imagine a zipper from pelvis to chest, zipping everything up and in. Keeping it close to you. Energetically activated. Roll your shoulders up, back, then down so they rest in their homes. Arms are down by your sides, fingers spread wide and active. Chin is tucked slightly so that the crown of your head draws upward. Energy comes up through your toes, the front of your body, lifting you up and making you tall. Energy flowing down from your head, cascading down your back to ground you out through your heels. A full cycle of energy.

PRACTICE

Mountain Pose

1. Find a place for your meditation.
2. Set your timer for three, five, or seven minutes.
3. Find a place to rest your gaze during your meditation and let your eyes become soft (If you're feeling like you want a challenge, you can try this with your eyes closed, but balance becomes pretty difficult with eyes closed. Sometimes it's best to just pick a spot on the wall or a light switch or something non-distracting).
4. Breathe in and out three times to prepare for your meditation.
5. Set up your mountain pose using the cues provided.
6. Let yourself feel mountainous.
7. When your timer sounds, close your eyes and breathe for a moment letting yourself feel the effects of your practice.

5.5

Watching the Thought Stream

First, a word on thoughts. Thoughts are not emotions. One more time for the people in the back: *thoughts are not emotions*. We talked last week about how it's important to feel feelings and not suppress them or pretend they don't exist. Emotions have to be felt in order to be resolved. The same is *not* true for thoughts. Emotions live deep inside our body, you can feel sadness in your heart, your stomach, or your arms. Thoughts come from our minds. Thoughts are a conditioned way of seeing and interacting with the world. By conditioned, I mean that someone at some point taught you. Thoughts are merely surface level. When you look deeply into the nature of something then you are going beyond the layer of the mind. Beyond stories, fears, expectations. Beyond words. There's a great TED Talk by Steven Hayes called 'Mental Brakes to Avoid Mental Breaks' and he talks about how everyone you meet adds to your mental framework whether you realize it or not and whether you want them to or not.

Imagine you're the mechanic for a building and you have a set of blueprints. Your blueprints came from your company, and you have no reason to question them. So you go to work, but things just aren't adding up. Nothing is where it's supposed to be, and you get more and more frustrated. You're forced to come to the conclusion that the blueprints you have are just not correct for this building, so you chuck the blueprints and work with what you can see. The company sends you new blueprints, you start working and quickly realize they're still wrong. You get new blueprints, they seem correct at first but then you realize that parts are still wrong. And so on and so forth. Sometimes it's accurate, sometimes it's not. You don't know which is which until you compare to the building in front of you. The blueprints are your thoughts, and the building is your life. You are responsible for your life regardless of the accuracy of your thoughts. Sometimes you might have to chuck the blueprint and just go with what's right in front of you.

Thoughts tell you that you already know what's going on, what it means for you, and how you should respond to it. Thoughts keep you from seeing the present moment for what it truly is. The present moment gets distorted by past experiences and worries about the future. Eckhart Tolle wrote in his book *The Power of Now* that the goal of mindfulness is to create a gap in the thought stream. In this gap is the chance to respond, not react, to what's really happening and not some distorted Picasso of a situation. If you aren't seeing a situation clearly, how can you expect to respond to it in a helpful way? Sometimes thoughts can even be true and still unhelpful. Then you have to ask yourself, would you rather be right, or would you rather be helpful? It's technically correct that people should be kind, that it's valid to get upset when someone mistreats you, that you shouldn't have to do the dishes all the time. Are those helpful thoughts? Or do they only serve to make you upset, creating a bigger issue than necessary?

Some thoughts are also just straight up false. I like to tell my clients that we all have an internal heckler. In yogic philosophy it's called the ego. For whatever reason we all have a critical internal voice, and it feeds us all the same two stories disguised in various ways. Those two stories are: you're doing something wrong, and you're not doing enough. If you see this story in any of its forms, you can just disregard it. It's a lie. You are exactly enough. You are doing the best that you can do. You are perfectly equipped to deal with your life. Anything else is ego. It's a lie. Feel free to throw it away. These thoughts will not improve your life. They will not make you a better person. They will not serve you well. Once you get used to observing your thoughts, you'll start to notice the same stories replay, sometimes ad nauseum. If you were X, they would love you more. They're unhappy because you can't do anything right. You're a burden. No one actually likes you. So on and so forth. The thoughts come and the thoughts go. They really only have the power that you give them. You don't have to believe them. You don't even have to call them yours. You are not your thoughts. Your thoughts come in, and unless you hold on to them, your thoughts go out.

PRACTICE

Watching the Thought Stream

1. Find a space to meditate and sit, stand, or lie down.
2. Set your timer for ten minutes.
3. Close your eyes and breathe in and out three times to prepare for your meditation.
4. See yourself sitting, lying, or standing by a riverbank, watching the water flow by.
5. See your thoughts in the stream, maybe as fish, eddies, or leaves on the surface.
6. There go your plans for dinner tonight, your worries about money or your car, your judgment that you're doing this wrong.
7. Every thought you have drifts slowly by while you watch from a distance, comfortably, beside the riverbank.
8. When your timer sounds, release the visualization. Breath for a moment. Notice the effects of your practice.

5.6

Child's Pose Meditation

Child's pose, Sanskrit: balasana, is a resting pose. If you've spent any time with kids, this might seem strange to you, but think of this more like 'sleeping baby pose'. The essence of the posture is to let go of any tension and just let yourself be completely held by the earth. Your entire weight being supported and comforted by the firm foundation beneath you. The vulnerability of letting down the defenses is...well, it's just terrifying. The world is a dangerous, hurtful, and scary place. Becoming vulnerable and defenseless isn't safe, right? You are partly correct. There is wisdom in recognizing when you are safe and when you need defenses. You are safe on your yoga mat. You are safe in your meditation. You are safe in mindful walking. Keeping up defenses during these times only hinders your practice. Working on this type of wisdom will serve you not only in your meditation but also in your life (especially in relationships with other people). There is power in recognizing when you feel unsafe. Vulnerability is uncomfortable. Vulnerability means you can be hurt.

Remember that it is your brain's literal job to keep you from getting hurt. If you've been hurt before then your brain is going to think that similar situations are also going to hurt you. What happens when your brain thinks you're going to get hurt? You get defensive. That's right – cue fight, flight, or freeze. Some people wear perfectionism like a suit of armor to protect them. If I'm X enough, I won't be judged, criticized, or feel unworthy (for more on this, see the wonderful work of Brené Brown). When we get defensive, we shut people out. Vulnerability is the only way to have a relationship. You have to be vulnerable to let people in. Imagine yourself like a castle surrounded by a tall wall that goes all the way around, with a moat and a drawbridge. If you're feeling spunky maybe throw a few alligators in there. The moment you sense that something might be painful (someone gets angry at you, someone touches you in a way that brings up a trauma, there's a conflict that needs resolved, etc), then the drawbridge closes. The windows get boarded up. Maybe the guards point their bows with flaming arrows. Maybe you've learned that pain comes when you least expect it, so you live your whole life under threat of attack. This is no way to live life. You are safe sometimes. Life also hurts sometimes. The point is, if you live your life always afraid of being hurt then you miss out on all the beautiful parts too. So, if only in your child's pose, let, yourself be defenseless. Let yourself be held.

PRACTICE

Sleeping Child

1. Find a quiet, comfortable space for your meditation.
2. You can lay face down or start on hands and knees. Bring your knees wide and your big toes to touch. Shift your hips back onto your feet and lower your chest to the ground. Rest your forehead. Arms stretched out in front of you, or elbows bent, and hands stacked to make a pillow for your forehead.
3. Take a moment to make sure you're comfortable – feel free to use any blankets, pillows, or yoga blocks as needed.
4. Start your timer for five or seven minutes.
5. Close your eyes and breathe.
6. With every exhale release more weight into the ground. Become heavy.
7. Feel held by the support of the earth. You are safe.
8. When your timer sounds, come to a seated position and breath. Notice the effects of your practice.

5.7

Tree Visualization

In Christianity, there is the parable of the wise and foolish builders. The foolish man built his house on the sand and when the storm came his house fell down because the sand underneath shifted and did not support the house. The wise builder built his house on a firm foundation of rock. When the storm came, his house stood unphased and was not moved because the foundation was solid. There is a similar message in yogic philosophy which is often termed 'root to rise'. Before standing up, shifting onto one foot, or really doing anything with the upper body, a yoga instructor will often cue the students to check in with their feet. The idea is to ensure that you feel stable and are connected with your foundation before you do anything in the upper body. Stability first, everything else follows.

Plants already know this. Plants start out as seeds. They are buried in the earth, and before they pop out as little saplings or flowers, first they develop a root system. The roots have several functions: transporting water and nutrients and anchoring the plant into the ground. Imagine a plant without roots. Let's make it an oak tree. Northern red oak trees are pretty common in the northeast United States and typically grow 60 to 75 feet tall. Without roots, the oak tree could never have survived to grow big and tall. It would have been taken out by a storm, a gust of wind, or just a normal winter. Without a foundation it's not only freak events that could wipe out the tree, a normal experience would be too much for it to handle. Trees are a beautiful example of the need to balance strength and flexibility. Trees are undeniably strong. They are solid and tall. They are firm and supportive. They also survive in part because they are flexible. They bend with the wind. That which is inflexible, breaks. The same is true for your mind.

PRACTICE

Tree Visualization

1. Find a place for your meditation – it is best to be standing or sitting.
2. Set your timer for five or seven minutes.
3. Close your eyes and breathe in and out to prepare for your practice.
4. See yourself as a tree – straight, solid, supported from beneath for maximum growth.
5. On your exhale, feel your foundation.
6. On your inhale, feel yourself expand.
7. See your thoughts, as leaves, rustling in the wind. The outermost layers. The surface layers.
8. Connect with the strength and flexibility that exist underneath.
9. Maintain a slow, steady, intentional breath cycle.
10. When your timer sounds, release the visualization. Blink your eyes open. Notice the effects of your meditation.

Week 6

Breath Plus...

Because breath is always available, it makes a pretty great foundation for a bunch of different meditative practices. Breath is the connection between mind and body. When breathing mindfully, body and mind are unified. They are one. This connection between mind and body is the starting place for any meditation. It is always a good idea to start a mindfulness or meditation practice with at least three rounds of mindful breathing. I think about this like a clearing. All day there are thoughts, situations, memories, expectations, worries, to do lists, conversations. These things buzz around in the brain like a swarm of bees, incessant white noise blocking you from being able to receive anything else. The mindful breathing at the beginning of the practice clears away the white noise so that you can receive what your meditation has for you. Mindful breathing makes you available to the present moment. Available to hear the intuition that would otherwise be drowned out by white noise.

Mindful breathing is also a good reminder that you are not your thoughts. Some people use the word 'disidentifying' which basically means that you are creating a separation between yourself and your thoughts. Your thoughts are not included in your sense of self, your identity. This process is not to be confused with dissociating, the mental health symptom, which is a shutting out and disconnection from thoughts, memories, identity, surroundings, and feelings. Creating a separation between sense of self and thoughts is different from blocking something out and living in the delusion that it doesn't exist. Interestingly enough, research and practice have shown mindfulness as an effective treatment to reduce dissociation as a trauma response. Typically, people dissociate because something is so overwhelming that the brain shuts down. Kind of like an electrical board that short circuits. By creating space and having a serene encounter with fear, memories, thoughts, and surroundings, the brain is no longer overwhelmed and does not shut down or dissociate. As a balance practice, creating space between self and thoughts is healthy, but dissociating from thoughts is unbalanced and disharmonious.

Breath is a helpful start to meditation, and it's also a great foundation for building. It is easy to start with breathing. Noticing the breath. Watching the flow. Connecting mind and body. Then layering on counting, pauses, or words. You can even guide breath in different ways throughout the body. Visualizations, energetic flow, and progressive muscle relaxations are also ways of layering onto a breath practice. When meditating, it is also helpful to come back to the breath whenever a distraction carries you away. Meditation teachers will often refer to breath as an anchor because it helps keep you in the meditation and not drifting away with any passing thought. Maintaining a steady, deliberate, deep breath regulates your body's stress response so that as long as you maintain your breath your body will remain in a state of calm relaxation. Your thoughts and fears can whip around you like wild winds in a ferocious storm, but your mindful breathing keeps you safe and peaceful.

6.1

Flower...Fresh

The next four practices are traditionally taught together as a pebble meditation. You find four pebbles, assign one to represent each of the four elements (flower, mountain, lake, space) then you complete three cycles of breath with each pebble. Picking one up, doing three cycles of breath with the mantra, then placing the pebble down. I'm going to go through each one separately to spend some quality time understanding the significance and meaning of each of the elements. You are, of course, more than welcome to do all four together whenever the mood strikes you. Much as I am honored to be your guide on this eight-week journey, I sincerely hope that you break free of the mold and practice in whatever way feels right to you.

The essence of a flower is freshness. To be fresh is to greet every moment as a potential for beauty, connection, and enlightenment. To be fresh is to not allow previous experience to cloud your current experience. Every moment you are completely washed and renewed. Think about the word 'renew'. It means to become new again – to have no expectations or conditioning. It's easy to get caught up in the routine of daily living – doing the same thing day after day. It's important to stay fresh and let every moment be new because otherwise it's easy to believe every moment and every person is just the same as all the others. How sad it would be to live with that belief. A flower blooms beautiful and full no matter what the world around it is doing. When you breathe in to smell a flower, you become fully enveloped in the experience. Every part of you is filled with the smell of the flower. Flowers are beautiful and full of life. When you breathe and repeat the mantra, you let yourself become new like a beautiful flower. You shed the old beliefs and shake off the feelings from the past. You are fresh.

PRACTICE

Flower...Fresh

1. Find a place for your meditation.
2. Close your eyes and breathe in and out to prepare for your practice.
3. As you breathe in, say silently to yourself: breathing in, I see myself as a flower.
4. As you breathe out, say to yourself: Breathing out, I feel fresh.
5. Breathing in, I see myself as a flower.
6. Breathing out, I feel fresh.
7. You might shorten to: Flower (inhale)...Fresh (exhale).
8. Continue until your practice feels complete.
9. Release the practice and breathe. Notice the effects of your practice.

6.2

Mountain...Strong

Mountains are a beautiful representation of strength, stability, and fortitude. There are mountains that have stood since the beginning of the earth. One of the things that I like best about mountains is that they don't care what goes on around them. During the winter, they are covered in snow. Spring comes and melts the snow. There are crisp, clear mountain streams that cut a path across their surface and countless animals birthed and living on their slopes. Trees grow and blossom. Summer comes and with it, the hikers – trekking up and down. Fall arrives and the leaves die, the hikers go home, and the animals take shelter for the coming winter. Years come and go. The mountain stands unchanged beneath the shifting surface activity.

Just like that mountain, you are so much more than the shifting surface of thoughts, activities, and emotions. Underneath all of that is who you truly are. When things stay the same we tend to overlook them, preferring to spend attention on the things that are changing. There are parts of you that deserve attention, perhaps for the very reason that they are immovable and unchanging. If you feel confused or chaotic, come back to those places of yourself that are stable. Your love of nail polish or clouds. Washing dishes or taking a shower. When you feel lost, remember that you have the compass. Life exists in cycles. Things come together and things fall apart. Snow falls and snow melts. There is birth. There is death. The mountain exists in quiet beauty. So can you.

PRACTICE

Mountain...Strong

1. Find a place for your practice.
2. Breathe in and out three times to prepare body and mind for meditation.
3. Breathing in, I see myself as a mountain.
4. Breathing out, I feel strong (feel free to substitute – stable, firm, grounded, etc).
5. You may choose to shorten to: Mountain (inhale)...Strong (exhale).
6. Continue until you feel satisfied.
7. Release the meditation. Breathe in and out. Observe the effects.

6.3

Water...See

You are standing by the shore of a huge lake. The surface is completely still, not a single ripple. The water is clear. Looking at the surface you can see the whole world reflected perfectly. You see clouds, birds flying overhead, trees, bright blue sky, and the mountains that surround the lake. Looking into its depths you see fish, stones on the bottom, and seaweed swaying gently with the movement of the water. Suddenly, a duck lands on the surface of the lake by where you're standing, and everything goes away. Mud is kicked up from the bottom and you can't see the fish or the pebbles. The surface is made of ripples and splashing, and you can no longer see anything reflected there. You wait. After a while, the reflection and clarity are restored, and you can see everything just as clearly as before. Imagine if you had tried to restore the stillness by jumping in the water and trying to smooth it out or push the mud back down. Rather than solve the issue, you would only have prolonged the time it takes to restore itself. So it is with you.

We have a gut instinct to jump into action mode to solve a problem. Something makes us uncomfortable or our brain labels something as a 'problem' so we immediately rush into trying to make changes to fix it. This works sometimes. If a baby is falling off a chair, by all means rush to catch the falling baby. There are situations that require correction and urgency. Not all situations are those situations. In fact, what if those situations are the rare exception? Could you accept that? If you believe that stress, worry, emotions (happy, sad, scared, angry, excited, etc), expectations, and thoughts distort the perception of reality, then wouldn't it make sense that stillness is the key to clarity? Your mind is that pond. Anger is a duck landing on the surface.

Everything is distorted and the reality of things is not clear. Sitting in silence and practicing mindful breathing restores the stillness that brings deep awareness and understanding. Rushing to action will only bring more chaos. Choices based on distorted reality are more likely to cause further damage. It would be like trying to do a paint by numbers if all the numbers got changed. You don't have the correct information to make the best decisions. So sit and trust that all will be revealed in its own time.

PRACTICE

Still water...I See

1. Find a place to practice; sit, stand, or lie down.
2. Breathe in and out several times to prepare yourself for meditation.
3. Inhale and say silently to yourself, 'breathing in, I see myself as still water'.
4. Exhale and say to yourself, 'breathing out, I see things as they truly are'.
5. Repeat this for a while. Inhale: Still water; Exhale: I see.
6. Release your practice and observe any changes in your body and mind.

6.4

Space...Free

I have a Facebook meditation group where I post information, quotes, and the schedule for free meditation classes. I posted a poll on there asking people what stops them from being happy. I gave some options – stress, worry, sadness, anger – but left it open so that people could add their own options too. Well, to my initial dismay someone added the option 'other people' and a few other people voted for that option. I thought to myself, 'don't these people know that other people aren't responsible for your emotions?' and I had to answer myself that, honestly, they probably don't. As a society, we live with the belief that other people cause our emotional reactions. That we are powerless, the emotions that come and go are a result of other people's actions. I can't control other people and I can't control my emotions to them; therefore, I cannot control my emotions. What a sad, powerless way to live. And so unnecessary. I truly believe that mindfulness is an empowerment practice. Take back the power from your thoughts. Take back the power from your emotions. Take back the power from your past experiences. It all belongs to you. The real you.

Remember how I said that Buddhist psychology sees the mental landscape like a garden? Inside you there are seeds of anger, sadness, insecurity, defensiveness, aggression, prejudice, and so forth. There are also seeds of happiness, joy, love, acceptance, etc. but they are less important to this conversation. It is possible for other people to influence the environment, but the seed of anger is within you. Someone may water it with unkind words, triggering language, or their own anger, but your experience of anger is from the seed of anger that exists within you. If you were to sit in stillness and look deeply into the nature of your anger, what do you think you would see? That person's face? Maybe at first. But what if you sat with it longer. Buddhist monk Thich Nhat Hanh said that the only condition for happiness is freedom. Freedom from mental clinging. Freedom from wrong perceptions. Freedom from cravings. This is a practice of happiness because it is a practice of freedom. Create space. Create freedom. Create happiness.

PRACTICE

Space...Free

1. Find a place for your meditation.
2. Breathe in and out three times to make yourself available to your practice.
3. As you inhale, say silently to yourself: 'breathing in, I see myself as never-ending space'.
4. As you exhale, say silently to yourself: 'breathing out, I feel free'.
5. Space. Free.
6. Continue until you are fully satisfied.
7. Release the practice and enjoy noticing the effects.

6.5

I am Home

Home. Home is the place where you belong. The place where you are safe, understood, and appreciated. Home is a place where you get to be completely yourself without fear of being rejected or criticized. Home is that perfect place in time and space that is meant just for you. Home isn't the building where you grew up. For most of us, childhood felt nothing like the utopia that I just described. It's okay if you can't even recall a time that you ever felt totally comfortable and accepted. Humans are social creatures. We are built for connection, yet somehow, we don't even know how to truly connect with ourselves let alone each other. The Zen practitioners believe that enlightenment is the realization that separateness is an illusion. That despite our distinct bodies, we are all connected. Home is a place of connection. Every moment is a chance for you to come home to yourself – your body, your breath, your existence. You are home. You have arrived.

To me, shame is the opposite of home. Shame says you don't belong. You are wrong. You are unworthy. Shame is ego. That voice of separateness in us all that says you're doing the wrong thing and you're not doing enough. Have you ever felt like everything you do is wrong? Or, that no matter how hard you try, you can never do or be enough? That is ego. That is shame. It's a lie, but it's such a hurtful lie that we don't even sit with it long enough to realize that it's a lie. Think about it, anytime a hurtful thought comes in, we tense up around it and we try to think about something else. But we believe it. We get hooked by the stories of insecurity, unworthiness, and insufficiency. Come home to yourself in these moments and breathe in the security of knowing that in every moment you are enough. You are exactly adequate for whatever life has in store for you. You are not alone. You are connected to the whole universe. You are home.

PRACTICE

I am Home

1. Choose to do this as a walking or still meditation.
2. Set your timer for five minutes.
3. Close your eyes and breathe several times to prepare your mind for your practice.
4. With every inhale say to yourself, "I am home...home... home..."
5. With the exhale, "I have arrived...arrived...arrived..."
6. Let yourself be filled with total presence and acceptance for yourself in this moment.
7. I am home.
8. I have arrived.
9. Continue until the timer sounds.
10. Release the practice and let yourself enjoy the effects of your meditation.

6.6

Gather and Clear

I'll be honest. This is one of my favorite practices. It's so versatile and so effective that once I learned it, it quickly became one of my go-to breathing techniques. This is your chance to take control as the gardener of your mind. We all have seeds of anger, resentment, sensitivity, judgment, insecurity, sadness, and worry inside of us. Sometimes life cultivates these seeds so that they overtake the rest of the garden. It's time to clear that away. You don't need it. It doesn't make your life better. You know what does make your life better? Love, joy, peace, patience, kindness, goodness, faithfulness, gentleness, and self-control. These are the seeds in your garden that deserve your attention and tender care. Life might not always water these seeds naturally, so it's your job to do it. A popular psychotherapy, dialectical behavior therapy, has a motto for clients, 'You may not have caused all the problems in your life, but you are the one responsible for fixing them'. Now is your opportunity to take control and decide what you want to gather and what you want to clear.

This practice is an awesome example of the necessity to use mindful meditation practices as part of a routine and on the go. You may notice that you have a habit of responding with anger, defensiveness, or criticism. It might be good to use those regularly in your practice. Maybe it's part of your daily morning meditation to undo some of the conditioning that life has thrown at you over the years. Awesome. More power to you. This practice is also really great to just use on the go when you feel someone or something watering a seed in you that you'd rather not have grow. Perhaps someone waters a seed of prejudice, self-doubt, or harshness in you. You notice it. Use your mindful breathing in the moment to redirect your focus and intention toward your goal.

PRACTICE

Gather and Clear

1. Find yourself where you are.
2. Close your eyes.
3. Decide what you want more of and what you want to get rid of.
4. Breathe in and out with intention.
5. With every inhale, visualize yourself taking in what you need.
6. With every exhale, see yourself gather what you've chosen from inside you and expel it with your breath.
7. Breathing in what you need.
8. Rooting out what you're getting rid of. Get it out of every nook and cranny of your being.
9. When the practice feels complete, release it.
10. Breathe normally for a few cycles and notice the effects of your practice.

6.7

Sun Breath

This is a practice of connecting breath to movement. A powerful way of connecting mind and body is using breath to move your body in rhythm. It's so graceful. It's like dance for non-dancers. Embodied movement describes a state of awareness that is completely in the body. No thoughts. Just breath and movement. There's a freedom in this state of non-thinking. You get to just be. There are lots of ways to do this: yoga, dance, fishing, horseback riding, skydiving, and aikido are just a few examples. People say 'thoughtless' like it's an insult, but what if it were a compliment? What if we actually valued time that was not spent in thinking? Usually when people say 'thoughtless' what they really mean is lack of awareness, which is more like living on autopilot. Thoughtlessness in this sense is being so completely in the present, moment to moment, that no thoughts exist. All that exists is pure, nonjudgmental experience.

I'm not really sure that 'sun breath' is the official name for this practice, but it's the name that I like. You start by standing (maybe run through the mountain pose guide from last week). With the inhale, sweep your arms out, to the side, and up until your palms meet over your head. Feel free to add a little backbend if it feels good. On the exhale, bring your hands together in front of your heart. The inhale is the rising of the sun – gathering energy. The exhale is the setting of the sun when all that energy comes back to you. With every inhale you are collecting energy and with every exhale you're bringing all that energy back home. If you like the visualization, feel free to use it. If you don't, don't. The power of these practices is not in your ability to follow instructions. The power of these practices comes from your ability to create a sense of home in yourself.

PRACTICE

Sun Breath

1. Find a place with enough space to practice.
2. I recommend standing, but you could also do this sitting or lying down.
3. Breathe in and out three times to make yourself available to your practice.
4. Inhale and sweep your arms out and up, palms meeting over your head.
5. Exhale and bring your hands to your heart, bring all the energy back in.
6. Complete 5-10 cycles.
7. Leave your hands at your heart and breathe normally for a while.
8. Notice the effects of your practice.

Week 7

Chakras

I have come to believe that my purpose in life is to understand things to help other people understand them and improve their lives. I truly believe that understanding and awareness are the key to making change. You probably read 'Chakras' and had one of two reactions: 'Oh my goodness, yes! I'm so excited' or 'I was with you up until you said chakras...'. Both are wonderful! Stick with me here. Chakras are traditionally believed to be hubs of different types of energy along the spine. They can be over or under active, each causing a variety of symptoms depending on the chakra. The practice is to balance and align all the chakras for optimal physical and mental functioning. You may recall that life energy, Prana, is believed to travel up and down the spine, so imbalances in the chakra would then cause impaired movement of Prana throughout the body. You can choose to believe this or not. What most people don't know is that the chakras correspond to Maslow's hierarchy of needs developed around 1940 and used to explain human motivation and functioning.

Abraham Maslow was an American psychologist who theorized that human needs are not all equal and that certain needs must be met before others. There are seven tiers of needs. There are also seven chakras. Coincidence? I think not. The seven chakras are loosely related to stability, passion, strength, acceptance, communication, seeing, and understanding. Maslow's seven tiers of needs are physiological needs, safety, sense of security, social needs, self-esteem, noticing beauty and art, and self-actualization. While perhaps not a 1:1 correspondence, the similarities are remarkable. Whether you ask a 20th century psychologist or a yogi from

500 BC, both will tell you that humans must first establish a sense of safety, followed by belonging then knowledge then limitless connection. It might seem pretty amazing that people from such different cultures, time periods, and educational backgrounds would stumble on the same theory of human functioning. If you really think about it, though, I bet it makes sense to you too. I say all of this for two reasons. First: don't discount chakras just because it seems like yogic nonsense. Let it be just helpful symbolism. Second: you may be surprised where you can find similarities. Don't stop looking.

This week we'll move through each chakra individually. I'll provide some information about the traditions because each is associated with a sound for chanting, a place in the spine, and a color. I will also lead you through what it might look like if it's either over or under active. The practice will be a visualization paired with breathing, for the purpose of bringing the energy back into balance. Remember, if chakras aren't your thing, you can always just follow along as a helpful metaphor rather than committing to the belief that it is scientifically valid. Discussions about chakras are also a good time to build up your storehouse of positive affirmations and reminders for yourself when you're having a hard time.

7.1

Root

In Sanskrit, the root chakra is called the Muladhara chakra. It sits at the very base of your spine. When you're sitting, it's the part of your body that's connected to the earth (anatomical location: perineum). The sound for chanting is Lam, and the color is a deep, scarlet red. The root chakra is the seat of safety, security, and stability. I sometimes called it the seat of anxiety. If it's imbalanced you might feel stressed, low self-esteem, constipated, under or overweight, insecure, and/or anemic. When the root chakra is balanced you have healthy digestion, a sense of groundedness and stability, and you are humble and energetic. Some good affirmations (or mantras if you prefer the term) are: I am safe, I am stable, I am grounded, I am balanced, I have everything I need, and I am worthy. Feel free to use one of these statements in your meditation practice.

As I mentioned, Abraham Maslow also theorized that physiological safety is required before any social or mental health work will be appropriate or effective. Physiological needs include protection from harsh weather, adequate food and water, sex (debatable, but Maslow did learn from Freud...), sleep, and protection from predators. It's important to note that money features prominently in almost all of these basic human needs. If a person doesn't have money, or is afraid that they won't have money, or if they do not have financial independence then this safety need is not met. In our society, money equals safety. Note: this need is more basic than your need for a relationship, so it may be tempting for your brain to prioritize feeling safe (notice I didn't say being safe – distortions exist!) over maintaining even a healthy and functional relationship. Just as Maslow observed that individuals cannot improve socially or mentally without satisfying safety needs, the teaching for the root chakra is 'I cannot grow from an unsteady foundation'. Your sense of stability, safety, and balance are the foundation. All else stems from this.

PRACTICE

Root Chakra Visualization

1. Find a calm, quiet, comfortable place for a seated meditation.
2. Set your timer for five minutes.
3. Close your eyes and breathe in and out to become available.
4. Imagine a red ball of light sitting at the bottom of your spine, at the place where your butt sits on the ground.
5. With every inhale, let the ball of light grow bigger and brighter.
6. With every exhale, see the red light growing smaller and dim.
7. Observe this process for a little while.
8. If you want, choose an affirmation to layer on.
9. Inhale – ball of light grows and brightens, and say to yourself, 'I am'.
10. Exhale – ball of light shrinks and dims while you say to yourself, 'safe' or 'balanced' or whatever else you choose.
11. Continue until your timer sounds.
12. Release the visualization.
13. Observe the effects of your practice.

7.2

Sacral

The Sanskrit name for the sacral chakra is Svadhisthana. Typically referred to as the seat of passion or creativity, the sacral chakra sits about two inches below your belly button and its color is orange. The sound for chanting is Vam. When out of balance you feel: guilty, shy, and irresponsible. You would also experience infertility, sexual dysfunction, allergies, and/or an eating disorder. When balanced you are able to enjoy sexual activity and you feel creative, joyful, passionate, prosperous, and patient. Some good affirmations are: I am creative, I am passionate, I am inspired, I am in control, I am unique, I am joyful, or simply, I feel.

The lesson from the sacral chakra is, I honor others but not before myself. Let's talk about boundaries. This word gets thrown around a lot in mental health circles and social media. Essentially, a boundary is just a point of separation between two things. There's a boundary between North and South Korea. There's a boundary between Maryland and Pennsylvania. They don't look anything alike because the purpose and expectations are different. And why are the purpose and expectations different? Because the relationship is different. Boundaries are always a balance between protection and connection, and they *should* look different based on the relationship. Having expectations for how people should treat you is not optional. We protect the things we value. By not having boundaries, you are sending yourself the message that you are not worth protecting. You deserve better than that. Your body will tell you when you're not comfortable with something. You've spent the last six weeks practicing listening to your body. When you notice that you're feeling out of balance, listen. Look deeply into the nature of this imbalance. You're not looking for blame or judgment. You're looking for neglected fences that need mending.

PRACTICE

Sacral Chakra Visualization

1. Find a place to practice.
2. Set your timer for five minutes.
3. Close your eyes and breathe to create space.
4. See a ball of orange light sitting in between your naval and your pelvis.
5. With every inhale, the light grows bigger and brighter.
6. With every exhale, the light becomes small and dim.
7. Observe the light for a little while.
8. Feel free to layer on an affirmation if that feels good to you.
9. Continue the practice until your timer sounds.
10. Release the visualization. Breathe normally. Observe the effects of your meditation.

7.3

Solar Plexus

The traditional name for the solar plexus chakra is Manipura. It is the seat of power and represented by a yellow ball of light about two inches above your belly button. The sound for chanting is Ram. When out of balance, you feel: weak, tired, guilty, digestive and liver problems, worthless, self-doubt, and low self-esteem. When balanced you feel: confident, active, strong, fierce, powerful, energetic, and determined. Some appropriate affirmations are: I am strong. I am fierce. I am able. I am determined. I am capable. I have a purpose. I can do anything. I am ambitious. I am intelligent. I am powerful. I am a force of nature. The Manipura chakra teaches us that self-love starts when I accept all parts of myself.

I truly believe that mindful meditation is an empowerment practice. Empowerment is another one of those typical mental health or social justice words. It refers to anything that increases the ability of someone to control their life or claim their rights. You are not getting rid of anything. You are not gaining anything. You are simply bringing all things together in balance and harmony to reclaim your power as a force of nature. The Manipura chakra is in you. The energy for strength and ferocity is already in you. You're not creating it. You're just unblocking it. It's like an old box tucked away on a shelf all dusty and forgotten. Use your breath to dust it off, open it up, and unleash it on the world. Light the match. Watch it burn.

PRACTICE

Manipura Visualization

1. Find a place to practice.
2. Set your timer for five minutes.
3. Close your eyes.
4. Breathe in and out with conviction.
5. See a ball of yellow light sitting between your belly button and ribs.
6. Inhale and watch the light expand and get brighter.
7. Exhale and watch the light become small and dim.
8. Observe the light for a little while.
9. If it feels right, add an affirmation. If not, just breathe and watch the light.
10. Continue until your timer sounds.
11. Release the visualization. Breathe normally. Enjoy the effects of your practice.
12. Go be fierce.

7.4

Heart

The heart, Anahata, chakra is symbolized by a green ball of light seated – as the name suggests – at the heart. The chanting sound is Yam. Typically associated with acceptance, when the heart chakra is unbalanced, you feel critical, judgmental, jealous, lonely, demanding, cold or unfeeling, narcissistic, and may have heart or lung problems such as asthma. When the heart chakra is balanced you feel trusting, tolerant, open-hearted, compassionate, serene, and emotionally balanced. Some popular affirmations to balance the heart chakra are: I am loving. I accept myself. Love is all there is. I accept others. I am compassionate. I forgive. I am kind. I am cherished. I am needed. The heart chakra teaches us that when we love ourselves, loving others comes naturally.

The heart chakra is a beautiful example of the need for balance. The world is a hurtful place. Mindful meditation doesn't stop the world from being hurtful. In fact, that's not even the goal. To be hurt means you care. If you want to be a loving, compassionate, and caring person then you're going to be hurt. In order to feel you have to be sensitive. Think about it. If you lost all feeling in your hands, then you wouldn't get burned or pricked. But you also wouldn't feel the warmth of holding your loved one's hands or be able to complete delicate tasks. It's a challenging trade off but getting it 'right' isn't about eliminating pain. Getting it right means living your life to the fullest and being exactly who you are no matter how the world treats you. Living whole-heartedly is a brave and vulnerable journey. For more on whole-hearted living see the works of Brené Brown.

I said it was a balance, right? Living whole-heartedly and

being kind starts with you. It starts with protecting yourself, being kind to yourself, and having those boundaries that we talked about. Having a balanced heart means seeing things for how they truly are even if it's not how you want it to be. Other people can act judgmental, critical, distant, unforgiving, harsh, shaming, or condescending. While a mindfulness practice doesn't stop that from hurting, it does help you not take it personally. When you look deeply, you realize that the way someone treats you has more to do with their conditioning, wrong perceptions, or personal suffering. It's like I tell my clients, a happy and healthy person doesn't walk around making other people feel bad about themselves. You get hit by an arrow, but you don't have to keep stabbing yourself with it. The balance is this: be sensitive enough to feel, but not overly sensitive so that you take things personally or become fragile. It might be helpful to remind yourself that you don't achieve balance. It's a moving target and you just do your best to fall somewhere close.

PRACTICE

Anahata Chakra Visualization

1. Find a place to practice your meditation.
2. Set your timer for five minutes.
3. Close your eyes and breathe in and out to bring yourself into this moment.
4. See a ball of green light filling your chest.
5. Inhale and see the light expand and brighten.
6. Exhale and see the light shrink and darken.
7. Observe the light for a while.
8. Decide if you want to add an affirmation to this practice.
9. Continue until your timer sounds.
10. Release the visualization. Bring yourself back to this space. Notice the effects of your practice.

7.5

Throat

The throat, Vishuddha, chakra is symbolized as blue light in your throat. The chanting sound is Ham, and it is the seat of truth and communication. The throat chakra has really obvious differences between over and under active. When the throat chakra is underactive you feel shy, nervous, fear conflict, and have a feeble voice while an overactive throat chakra manifests as lying, arrogance, and aggression. Either imbalance can exist with difficulty listening and throat or thyroid conditions. With a balanced throat chakra, you feel truthful, able to express yourself confidently and assertively, peaceful, and able to communicate competently. Effective affirmations include: My voice matters. I have the words that I need. I express myself clearly. I have opinions. I take up for myself. I speak kindness. I speak love. My voice is strong. The throat chakra teaches us to always speak truth.

One of my favorite topics is communication. Communication is a goal-oriented behavior. The purpose is to get an idea from your head into someone else's head without it getting distorted. This takes skill because there are two filters here. First, the idea goes through your filter, where you translate it into words, tone, body language, etc. Next, it goes through the listener's filter, based on their perceptions, expectations, and experiences. When you know someone well, you start to account for their filter and communicate in ways that you think will make it more likely for them to understand. So, the first lesson of communication is this: you must communicate in a way that the other person can hear. The second lesson is: truth does not have to be harsh. Some people have the misperception that it's okay to speak harshly as long as it is disguised as 'being truthful'. This is false.

Sometimes it takes skill and forethought, but there is always a way to speak truth in such a way that it is not harsh. Whether the person feels hurt by it is another matter entirely. You cannot, I repeat, *cannot*, take responsibility for other peoples' emotional reactions. You can only do your best to create an environment where they feel safe and accepted.

There are four Buddhist practices for right speech. First, do not lie or be deceptive. Second, do not speak in a way that causes disharmony among people. Third, do not use harsh, rude, impolite, or abusive speech. Fourth, do not gossip. To a Christian ear, these should all sound familiar. Ephesians 4:29: *'Let no corrupt communication proceed out of your mouth, but that which is good to the use of edifying, that it may minister grace unto the hearers'* (4).

PRACTICE

Vishuddha Chakra Visualization

1. Find a place to practice and set a five minute timer.
2. Breathe in and out to make yourself available for your meditation.
3. See a bright blue ball of light filling your throat.
4. Inhale – the light shines brighter and grows bigger.
5. Exhale – the light shrinks and dims.
6. Observe the light for a little while.
7. Layer on an affirmation if it feels right.
8. Continue until your timer sounds.
9. Release the visualization. Breathe. Observe.

7.6

Third Eye

In Sanskrit, Ajna chakra is the seat of intuition that lies between the eyebrows. The color is a deep indigo blue and the sound for chanting is Om (or Aum depending on your philosophical bent). An unbalanced Ajna chakra shows itself as panic, fear, manipulation, distorted perceptions, lack of imagination and clarity, migraines, and nightmares. When your third eye is balanced, you feel intuitive, insightful, clear headed, mentally strong, spiritual, and serene. Effective affirmations for balancing the third eye are: I see clearly. I trust myself. I see things for how they truly are. I trust my decisions. I trust my intuition. I think clearly. I know the answer. The Ajna chakra teaches us to be open to exploring the things that we cannot see.

There is so much that gets in the way of seeing things for how they truly are. Sometimes our past clouds our present. We see the present moment through a lens that is dirty. Imagine wearing a pair of glasses that have the word 'unworthy' or 'failure' written on them. Everything you see will seem like it's telling you that you're unworthy or a failure, but that's not true to reality. Sometimes we are so afraid of getting hurt that we don't let ourselves be vulnerable enough to experience what life has to offer. We self-sabotage. Without realizing it, we make choices that confirm our fears. Our expectations, worries, insecurities, past hurts, or conditioning teach us to see and respond to things in a certain way. With the help of your intuition, you get the joy of clearing out all the garbage to make space for an overwhelming abundance of beautiful treasures. Think of it like mental spring cleaning!

PRACTICE

Third Eye Chakra Visualization

1. Find a place to practice.
2. Set your timer for three, five, or seven minutes.
3. Breathe in and out several times to prepare yourself for meditation.
4. See a ball of deep indigo blue light resting between your eyebrows.
5. Breathe in and let the light expand and brighten.
6. Breathe out and let the light become small and dim.
7. Observe the light for a while.
8. Layer on an affirmation if you want to.
9. Continue until your timer sounds.
10. Let the visualization fade. Breathe normally for a moment.
11. Observe the effects of your practice.

7.7

Crown

In Sanskrit, the crown chakra is called the Sahasrara chakra. It is represented as a ball of purple light floating a few inches above the very top of your head and it is the seat of connection and spirituality. The sound for chanting is silence or sometimes Om/ Aum. When the crown chakra is unbalanced, you feel apathy, disconnected, spiritual crisis, materialistic, fear, and problems with thinking and memory. When balanced, you feel peaceful, connected, and blessed. You also have wisdom, a sense of unity, and a strong nervous system. Affirmations to use are: I am divine. I understand. I am. I am light. I am at peace. I am enlightened. I know. The crown chakra teaches us that we are merely vessels for light and love.

Remember that this is the seventh step on the staircase to wellness. There is no skipping a step or jumping to the end. Maslow and the yogis agree – you have to fulfill and balance all the other needs before you are truly able to connect at a spiritual level. Connection must be without fear or insecurity. Connection without shame. Connection with boundaries. Connection without judgment or jealousy. Connection without domination or feebleness (Christians – notice I didn't say 'submission'). Connection without delusion. There is a unity at this level which is impossible if you are still hooked by these things. In fact, there's a *ton* of research on the effects of anxiety on relationships. Recall that anxiety lives in the root chakra where we get our sense of safety and stability. Anxiety is a primal pressure to solve a crisis, so resolving anxiety is even more important to your brain than maintaining relationships. With insight and awareness, it is possible to stop self-sabotaging. It is possible to recognize that you're hooked, to breathe with it, and let it be.

PRACTICE

Sahasrara Chakra Visualization

1. Find a place to meditate.
2. Set your timer for five or seven minutes.
3. Breathe in and out three times to become available for your practice.
4. See a ball of beautiful purple light floating above the top of your head.
5. Inhale and see the light grow and brighten to a blinding white.
6. Exhale and see the light shrink and dim to purple.
7. Observe the light for a little while.
8. Decide if you want to layer on an affirmation.
9. Continue until your timer sounds.
10. Let the visualization fade. Bring yourself back to this space.
11. Give yourself time to enjoy the effects of your practice.

Week 8

Creating Connections

I've read a lot of research on relationships. *A lot* of research. Like, enough research that if I stacked it all up it would be a toddler high. And not one of those skimpy toddlers, like a chunker of a toddler. The reason I say that is so you know that this discussion is the product of extensive research and not just my own limited experiences. Connection and relationship are basically synonyms, right? And attachment and relationship are basically synonyms, right? So, shouldn't attachment and connection be basically synonyms? They're not. Let's talk attachments first. There's this theory, attachment theory, that says we learn how to relate to others when we're really little. Our caregivers (parents, guardians, teachers, daycare providers, etc.) either consistently meet our needs and we can trust them, or they don't. If we have a secure attachment, then we trust people to meet our needs and we feel safe to explore and try new things. If the care is inconsistent – we aren't comforted when we're sad or scared, people aren't there when we need them – then we have one of two reactions: anxiety or avoidance. Anxious attachment is essentially abandonment issues – you get worried and upset when you think people might leave you, you want to be close to people when they're upset so you can keep an eye on them, conflict makes you really anxious, so you usually avoid it or freak out during it. Avoidant attachment is also not trusting people, but you get overly independent, don't let yourself be vulnerable, and totally just disengage during conflict. Attachment patterns develop early in childhood and typically are unchanged through adulthood. Psychologists talk about secure attachments as a necessity for security and growth. Buddhists talk about attachments as something to eliminate.

Who's right? Both.

Buddhists are not anti-relationship, quite the opposite, actually. The Buddhist meaning of attachment is more like clinging. Holding on to something even if it's harmful or not true to reality. Buddhists often use the term 'non-attachment' – non-attachment to outcome is doing something without being invested in any particular result, non-attachment to mental fixations means not being hooked by expectations, wrong beliefs, or emotions. This is very different from attachment as connection. Having a relationship based on connection rather than attachment means having a foundation of love, acceptance, and understanding. The other person is in your life solely because you want them there. Not because they 'complete' you. Not because you're scared to be alone. Not because being married is what you're supposed to be. The Gottmans are researchers who specialize in romantic partnerships, and they boast over 90% accuracy in predicting divorce. You know how they do it? They watch partners during conflict. The way couples interact during conflict is the single most accurate predictor of whether or not the relationship will last, and conflict is inevitable. Anytime you're in a relationship with someone, there will be conflict. Guaranteed. And guess what? That's when those attachment things rear their ugly heads. I read a research study that showed mindfulness actually reduces and can eliminate the negative effects of insecure attachment on relationships. Pretty cool, huh? There's a lot more research to be done, but it makes sense to me that a big part of that is the emphasis on connecting, but not attaching. We are partners together, but my sense of safety is not dependent on you. I will not lose my sense of peace because I might lose you. If it would happen, I would be devastated. But now I am calm. Our conflict is a chance to grow, not a threat to my safety.

8.1

Lotus Flower Hands

The lotus is a symbol of purity, enlightenment, and rebirth. There's a popular phrase, 'no mud, no lotus', which literally refers to the fact that lotuses are a water flower and have their roots in the mud. The phrase is used to represent the life lesson that out of the most difficult or 'dirty' experiences we are able to blossom into the most beautiful version of ourselves. There's a quote attributed to a Roman stoic philosopher, Musonius Rufus, that goes, *'If you accomplish something good with hard work, the labor passes quickly, but the good endures; if you do something shameful in pursuit of pleasure, the pleasure passes quickly, but the shame endures'* (5). We live so identified with our thoughts that we think that what our brain wants is what *we* want and that's not always true! Your brain wants what it has been conditioned to believe will result in the highest chance of pleasure. Short term gain. Remember, if you're not happy with the way your life is, then you need to do something different. Doing what you've always done is only going to get you what you're already getting.

As a society, we struggle with accepting short term loss even if there's long term gain. We want fast rewards. We also don't like sitting in discomfort. There's a balance here just like everything else. What's the point of making life more uncomfortable than it has to be? Some fixes are simple – if you're cold, get a blanket. If your partner misunderstood your intention, set the record straight (calmly and with kindness). Splurge every now and then. Have a lazy day. In no way am I saying that life should be nose to the grindstone 24/7/365. I'm saying that sometimes you have to choose to sit in discomfort because you know it's an investment. You breathe through sobs for 15 minutes because the alternative is self-harm, self-sabotage, or avoiding facing the feelings. You let yourself listen to the ego-laden emotional stories of not good enough or always doing wrong because you know you have to hear them in order to challenge and resolve them. You let yourself enjoy a fun-filled day with family even if your anxiety keeps creeping in and whispering, 'this might not last'. Patience means recognizing that things have to unfold in their own time. Trust that everything will work itself out and the best thing you can do is relax your body and be kind to yourself and others. That's what I learned in all my hours of research. The best thing for a person and for a relationship is to calm your body and be kind to yourself and others.

PRACTICE

Lotus Flower Hands

1. Decide to sit or stand.
2. Set your timer for five or seven minutes.
3. Close your eyes and breathe with intention.
4. Relax your shoulders and bring your hands to your heart with palms and fingers together.
5. Let your index, middle, and ring fingers separate and spread wide.
6. Thumbs, pinkies, and heel of the hands are together.
7. Thumbs are gently resting against your chest.
8. This is your own personal lotus flower.
9. Breathe in and out fully, letting yourself feel whatever you feel.
10. When your timer sounds, lower your hands.
11. Observe the effects of your meditation.

8.2

Intention Setting

A thing intended; an aim; a plan. Intention gives us direction. It's so easy to get caught up in the routine of daily life that we forget what we're living for. Existing on autopilot, we're not being an active participant in our life. On the other hand, the road to hell is paved with good intentions, as they say. It's easy to get up in the morning, sit in serenity with a cup of coffee and say to yourself, 'my intention is to live peacefully today'. Next thing you know you're driving to work, a car tails you, speeds around you, and cuts you off, then you're yelling enough profanity to make a sailor blush. Don't worry, we've all been there. What I mean to say is, more often than not, intentions go out the window because we forget about them and get lost on autopilot again. Intentions are beautiful because you get the chance to decide what you want for yourself. Do you want to be more curious? Notice more beauty around you? Speak love to everyone you meet? Accept whatever your body has in store for you? All wonderful intentions.

Intentions are the first step to participating in your life. Change happens in the present moment. Real change happens because you do something – in the present moment – differently than you've done before. You set the intention to see more beauty around you. Do you notice the birds in the sky or the trees on your drive to work? Do you notice the smile on the face of your coworker or the pattern on the floor of your office? What beautiful things are there for you to notice that you've overlooked? The power of intention comes from your ability to follow through. They call it 'practice' for a reason. You string together moments of awareness, each one like a beautiful pearl, and soon you've got a whole necklace, a whole life. Moment by moment. Use props if it helps you. Maybe every red light you see is a call to remember your intention. Every door you walk through or every time you look at the clock reminds you of the direction you've chosen for yourself.

PRACTICE

Intention Setting

1. Find a place to sit or stand.
2. Close your eyes and place one hand on your chest and one hand on your belly (or choose a different hand position – use your own intuition).
3. Breathe in and out three times to create space in your mind.
4. Continue to breathe fully and either set an intention for yourself or see if one comes naturally to you.
5. Don't let yourself effort. There is no right or wrong. Whatever comes up is perfect.
6. Feel your intention fill your whole body – filling your chest and spreading to your toes, your fingers, and out the top of your head.
7. Enjoy this moment.
8. When you feel complete (and maybe push yourself to stay a little longer than your mind tells you to) release the practice.
9. Notice any changes in your mind or body as a result of your meditation.

8.3

Love Is All There Is

At the first yoga studio I ever went to, I met my yoga mentor. She is a beautiful soul who spent a lot of time in India. I noticed that the guided meditation she led was almost always the same. It went something like this:

You are sitting firmly grounded and balanced. Your eyes are closed. Your spine is tall. Your shoulders are relaxed. Your hands are folded in the center of your lap. The crown of your head is lifting. Your tongue is curled back to the roof of your mouth. Observe your breath for a little while. (What seems like forever passes and then...) You are sitting on the very top of the tallest mountain. Top of the world. You see the earth laid out before you. The earth is drifting away, becoming smaller and smaller until it's just a tiny dot. Then, it is gone. You are at the center of the universe. All that surrounds you is love. As you breathe, repeat in your mind, 'baba nam kevalam' and ideate on the meaning: love is all there is. (What seems like forever passes and then...) slowly bring yourself back to this place and this time. Blink your eyes open.

She would usually guide this as a 15 minute meditation, and as you can see, the words took all of 30 seconds to say. Most of the time is spent in silent recitation of the mantra. This is a type of meditation practice called vipassana meditation. Vipassana meditation involves the repetition of a phrase silently to oneself for the purpose of producing insight, clear-sightedness, and mental fortitude. It is one of the most popular forms of meditation and some even believe it to be the only meditation practice with consistent benefits. I don't know about all that, but if it works, it works. There is no need to use the Sanskrit version or even to say 'love is all there is'. Meditators in some traditions argue that a mantra should only be given by your personal meditation teacher, but again, for our purposes, I don't see the need to be so strict. Feel free to consult with a mentor if you feel so inclined, otherwise go ahead and pick your own mantra. There are all kinds of resources if you want some guidance. If you're feeling stuck, just stick with love is all there is. It's a good place to start.

PRACTICE

Vipassana Meditation

1. Find a comfortable place to sit.
2. Set your timer for 15 minutes.
3. Observe your breath for a long while.
4. After several minutes, begin to repeat your selected phrase silently.
5. Continue until your timer sounds.
6. Release your practice. Breathe in and out several times.
7. Observe the effects of your practice.

8.4

Smile to Myself

This is one of those times that the same practice shows up in Eastern practice and contemporary mental health treatment. There's a coping strategy called the 'half smile exercise' which literally involves forming your face into a half smile and just breathing like that for a while. There's research that supports this exercise for improving mood and decreasing negative thinking. It's called a half smile because it should be a gentle upturn in the sides of your mouth. Making the smile exaggerated actually eliminates the benefits of the practice which I think is pretty significant. The usefulness of a smile comes from the gentle moment of kindness that you offer yourself, not straining to contort yourself into some particular shape. The Toaists teach that one should always carry an inward smile to oneself. The inner smile is in gratitude to your body and to carry you peacefully through life no matter what the external world brings.

Don't set yourself up for failure. Expectations are the enemy of progress because oftentimes our expectations for ourselves are not realistic. It goes a little something like this: learn something, get excited, set unreasonably high expectations for self, work hard for a while, don't reach goals, get disappointed in self, give up. This might even be you right now. Maybe you've been working faithfully the last seven and a half weeks, but you're still getting angry, having unkind thoughts, or acting impulsively. I have good news and bad news for you. You will never achieve an anger-free, impulse-free, life filled with only kind thoughts; however, with practice you will always make progress. If you expect to be able to meditate your way to eternal happiness, then I'm afraid you're going to be sorely disappointed. You will always experience the full range of human emotions. You will always feel pain, frustration, hopelessness, disappointment, and discomfort. There's no getting rid of these things. With practice, the feelings lose their power over you. You may not be able to get rid of anger, but you can stop trusting that your anger is reality. You don't have to believe the stories that your anger tells you. This is the fruit of your practice. So, smile to yourself. Even when you are angry, smile to yourself. Even if you don't reach your goal, smile to yourself.

PRACTICE

Half Smile

1. Sit, stand, or down.
2. Set your timer for three or five minutes.
3. Close your eyes and breathe in and out three times to create space in your mind.
4. Gently find yourself in a slight smile.
5. You might choose to call to mind an image that makes you smile (e.g. a loved one's face, a beach, a puppy, or a mountain cabin by a lake).
6. Rest here and enjoy your practice.
7. When your timer sounds, let your awareness drift through your body and observe any effects from your meditation.

This is an especially good practice to keep in your back pocket for an 'as needed' pick me up.

8.5

Observe

Humans have what I like to call 'emotional tunnel vision'. Scientists have actually done research to prove that when people are experiencing 'negative' emotions (anger, worry, stress, sadness, etc.) the brain literally notices fewer things. The attention is so focused on whatever the identified 'problem' is that the mind ignores everything else. The brain means well but sometimes doesn't go about things in the most helpful way. Let's talk stress. Stress is a synonym for pressure. Stress is when your brain is faced with something that it labels problematic and requires attention for a solution. Therefore, stress is literally the experience of pressuring yourself to solve a problem. There are some underlying assumptions here. What if the situation isn't actually problematic, and you're operating on a misperception? Chances are there's some false sense of urgency sprinkled in there. What if you can't do anything about the situation and it just needs to resolve itself in its own time?

Unless you have the presence of mind to recognize these distorted perceptions, your brain is going to keep sending out those stress messages to your body. You're going to keep pressuring yourself for a non-existent solution. You're also going to miss out on the wonderful things that life has to offer because your brain has tunnel-visioned onto the identified problem. So, while you're busy exhausting yourself unnecessarily, you're missing the birds singing, the sun shining, and the smiles on the faces of your loved ones. What a waste, right? You deserve better than that. Today's practice is simply to observe what exists. There is no need to do anything with it or create a story around it. You simply see what there is to see – you're seeing what's what, if you will. You are training yourself to be able to notice anything without feeling a need to respond, 'correct', or even have an opinion about it. Heads up, it's a lot more difficult than it seems like it would be. Challenge yourself to enjoy this as a practice of freedom.

PRACTICE

Observe

1. Find a place to meditate.
2. Set your timer for five, seven, or ten minutes.
3. Close your eyes and breathe in and out three times to become available.
4. Let your attention wander throughout your body and then to your mind.
5. Move slowly and notice all the tiny spaces you might normally overlook (joints, spaces between bones, individual toes and fingers) .
6. Challenge yourself to simply notice without changing or responding in any way.
7. If you feel complete before your timer sounds, let your attention rest on your breathing.
8. Watch it flow in. Watch it flow out. Your task is to let it be natural without altering it.
9. When your timer sounds, give yourself a few moments to enjoy the effects of your practice.

8.6

Listening for Guidance

Have you ever tried to think of something, and it seems like the harder you try, the farther away the thought gets, but as soon as you move on to something else, suddenly the thought pops in? Part of that is the emotional tunnel vision that we talked about yesterday. The more you pressure yourself for a solution, the less likely you are to think of one because you're so hyper focused on the problem. Having 100% of your attention on the problem means that you have 0% of your attention left to notice a solution. That's really just math. A calm and clear mind creates space for good ideas to come in. Imagine having a house filled with clutter. Even if someone stops by and offers you the most beautiful and comfortable couch, you wouldn't be able to accept it because you don't have any space! It's necessary to clear out the old, broken, useless clutter so that you can make room for better things. There's a whole universe filled with wisdom, love, and understanding just waiting to make a home inside of you. For the purpose of this practice, it doesn't matter whether you believe this is the universe sending you messages, God speaking to you, or your own inner wisdom coming through.

This is a special message for trauma survivors (abuse, neglect, violence, sexual assault, natural disaster, single event, long-term, a mix of a couple different things). Trauma turns the world upside down. When people hear posttraumatic stress disorder, usually the word that gets the attention is trauma. This is a trauma disorder, right? Well, yes, in part. PTSD is also a *stress* disorder. Literally your body has a confused stress response. There's so much research about the effects of trauma on a person's body, mind, soul, and relationships (for more, see the work of Bessel van der Kolk). It's devastating. One of the saddest things is that people who have been victimized are more likely to be revictimized. One theory is that when a person is victimized, they stop trusting their intuition. Essentially, if you've been hurt then you don't trust yourself to be able to keep yourself safe anymore. So, you ignore your gut. When you don't trust your gut, you ignore the messages that it sends about what's safe and unsafe, so you are more likely to find yourself in or to stay in an unsafe situation. Heartbreaking. You deserve better than that. It's time to reconnect with your intuition and build trust in yourself. Also, consider this your personal invitation to seek help. The PsychologyToday website has a 'find a provider' function to connect you easily to a mental health therapist. There is help.

PRACTICE

Listening for Guidance

1. Find a quiet, peaceful place to meditate (seated is recommended).
2. Close your eyes.
3. Let your hands rest in your lap or use the traditional mudra (hand position).
4. Mudra: put your middle and ring finger to the pad of your thumb and connect the tips of all five fingers to the fingers of the other hand. Turn your hands so your thumbs are on top, and your pinkies and index fingers are pointed down. Bring your pinkie to rest about two inches above your belly button. Relax your shoulders.
5. Breathe in and out to create space in the mind.
6. When you're ready, call to mind a difficulty in your life.
7. Stay rooted in this moment and let your mind stay spacious and calm.
8. Listen for guidance to drop in (it's okay if nothing happens).
9. When you feel complete release the practice, let your hands return to your lap.
10. Observe the effects of your practice.

8.7

Learning to Sit

It's time to put some pieces together. Recall in the working with emotions practices that we never once spent time deciding if emotions were 'valid' or not. There's a growing focus on the importance of validating your own emotions and validating the emotions of other people. That is partly correct. Validating emotions is an example of how we, as a society, swung from one extreme to the other and completely jumped over the helpful middle ground. It's unhelpful (and hurtful) to disregard your own and others' feelings. Consider phrases like: you'll get over it. No blood, no foul. Rub some dirt in it. And perhaps worst of all: I went through the same thing, you just have to get on with your life. A lot of us grew up having to make arguments for why our emotions were valid because otherwise they were disregarded. It's like we had a feeling and then we had to create a water-tight story for why that feeling deserved attention and empathy. Then, over a generation or so we swung to the other side where all feelings are valid AND deserve time, attention, and empathy.

All emotions are valid. Emotions also come and go (remember the clouds in the sky practice?). When we sit in an emotion – question it, come up with a story for why it is there, or try to rationalize it – then we're forcing it to stay longer than it needs to. Validating an emotion doesn't mean letting it stick and stay forever. Validating an emotion means that it doesn't have to stay. It can come and go. An emotion can exist without needing to have a story for why it's there and what makes it worthy to exist. What if you could let yourself be sad, angry, or happy and just let yourself feel. Emotions are often our guide for our behavior, so you say to yourself, 'unless I know this is an accurate emotion, how will I know how to act?' Consider that all emotions distort reality, that they are messengers with a message for you, but only by breathing in calmness and letting them come and go will you see clearly to take action (if action is even called for). Just let yourself sit with the feeling and breathe with it. Sometimes we cling to really uncomfortable emotions just because we feel some need to prove that they are valid. We create story after story for why we feel this awful way. Your practice is to let yourself feel any way that you want to without questioning its worthiness, without feeling the need to act on it, and without creating a story for its existence.

PRACTICE

Sit

1. Find a calm, peaceful, comfortable place to sit.
2. Set your timer for 15 minutes.
3. Close your eyes.
4. Breathe.
5. Keep yourself anchored by your breath, coming back to it whenever you get distracted.
6. Let noises come and go.
7. Let thoughts and emotions come and go.
8. Continue until your timer sounds.
9. Let your awareness drift throughout your body taking in the effects of your practice.

Where To Go from Here...

Societies are a reflection of the people who live in them. The same issues that plague society are present at the family and the individual level. Societies are chaotic because families are chaotic. Families are chaotic because individuals are chaotic. Individuals are chaotic because of all the things we've discussed over the last eight weeks – stress, conditioning, expectations, attachment, trauma, illness, loneliness, patterns of negative and distorted thinking, and just plain old inability to manage emotions. Humans are social beings, and we learn mostly by watching other people, so it's natural that chaotic patterns are passed from person to person and generation to generation until someone changes the pattern. There's a lot of talk right now about stopping the cycle. Maybe substance use is passed down in your family and you're courageous enough to stop the cycle. Maybe it's anger, violence, prejudice, or stress that's been passed down to you. Mindful meditation is a transformative practice. When you transform yourself then you naturally change all of your relationships and all of your interactions. There is power in being peaceful. There is power in smiling. There is power in being able to actually *be* instead of always feeling pressured to do. I'm not arrogant enough to believe I know what your personal calling is in this world. That's for you to figure out. Our journey over the last eight weeks has taken us through Japan, China, India, the United States, Rome, and across thousands of years. Everybody is saying the same thing: relax your body and be kind to yourself and others. That's how you change the world. It's like that old saying, 'it's not what you say, it's how you say it'. You have your own personal calling in this life. Do it. Be you. You have unique gifts and talents that the world needs. Do it with peace and kindness. That's where you go from here. This book and these practices are your springboard into living the best life you can live. Enjoy it.

Recommended Reading

The Art of Communicating by Thich Nhat Hanh

Meditation Is Not What You Think by Jon Kabat-Zinn

Wherever You Go, There You Are by Jon Kabat-Zinn

The Lost Art of Listening by Michael P. Nichols, PhD

Zen and the Art of Happiness by Chris Prentiss

Zen Mind, Beginner's Mind by Shunryu Suzuki

When Things Fall Apart by Pema Chodron

Start Where You Are by Pema Chodron

The Body Keeps the Score by Bessel van der Kolk

Braving the Wilderness by Brené Brown

The Gifts of Imperfection by Brené Brown

The Five Love Languages by Gary Chapman

The Science of Trust: Emotional Attunement for Couples by John Gottman

The 7 Principles for Making Marriage Work by John Gottman and Nan Silver

Endnotes

(1) Newton, I. (1675) *Sir Isaac Newton to Robert Hooke*. February 5, 1675 [Letter]. https://www.newtonproject.ox.ac.uk/view/texts/normalized/OTHE00101

(2) Laozi. (1988). Tao te ching (S. Mitchell, Trans. Chapter 67). New York: Harper Perennial. https://cpb-us-w2.wpmucdn.com/u.osu.edu/dist/5/25851/files/2016/02/taoteching-Stephen-Mitchell-translation-v9deoq.pdf

(3) Nhat Hanh, T. (1999) The heart of the Buddha's teaching: transforming suffering into peace, joy and liberation: the four noble truths, the noble eightfold path, and other basic Buddhist teachings (pp. 27). New York: Broadway Books

(4) Crossway Bibles. (2007). ESV: study Bible: English standard version. Wheaton, Ill, Crossway Bibles.

(5) Rufus, M. (n.d.) Fragment 51. https://philocyclevl.files.wordpress.com/2016/09/yale-classical-studies-10-cora-e-lutz-ed-musonius-rufus_-the-roman-socrates-yale-university-press-1947.pdf

O-BOOKS

SPIRITUALITY

O is a symbol of the world, of oneness and unity; this eye represents knowledge and insight. We publish titles on general spirituality and living a spiritual life. We aim to inform and help you on your own journey in this life.
If you have enjoyed this book, why not tell other readers by posting a review on your preferred book site?

Recent bestsellers from O-Books are:

Heart of Tantric Sex
Diana Richardson
Revealing Eastern secrets of deep love and intimacy to Western couples.
Paperback: 978-1-90381-637-0 ebook: 978-1-84694-637-0

Crystal Prescriptions
The A-Z guide to over 1,200 symptoms and their healing crystals
Judy Hall
The first in the popular series of eight books, this handy little guide is packed as tight as a pill-bottle with crystal remedies for ailments.
Paperback: 978-1-90504-740-6 ebook: 978-1-84694-629-5

Your Simple Path
Find Happiness in every step
Ian Tucker
A guide to helping us reconnect with what is really important in our lives.
Paperback: 978-1-78279-349-6 ebook: 978-1-78279-348-9

365 Days of Wisdom
Daily Messages To Inspire You Through The Year
Dadi Janki
Daily messages which cool the mind, warm the heart and guide you along your journey.
Paperback: 978-1-84694-863-3 ebook: 978-1-84694-864-0

Body of Wisdom
Women's Spiritual Power and How it Serves
Hilary Hart
Bringing together the dreams and experiences of women across the world with today's most visionary spiritual teachers.
Paperback: 978-1-78099-696-7 ebook: 978-1-78099-695-0

Dying to Be Free
From Enforced Secrecy to Near Death to True Transformation
Hannah Robinson
After an unexpected accident and near-death experience, Hannah Robinson found herself radically transforming her life, while a remarkable new insight altered her relationship with her father, a practising Catholic priest.
Paperback: 978-1-78535-254-6 ebook: 978-1-78535-255-3

The Ecology of the Soul
A Manual of Peace, Power and Personal Growth for Real People
in the Real World
Aidan Walker
Balance your own inner Ecology of the Soul to regain your
natural state of peace, power and wellbeing.
Paperback: 978-1-78279-850-7 ebook: 978-1-78279-849-1

Not I, Not other than I
The Life and Teachings of Russel Williams
Steve Taylor, Russel Williams
The miraculous life and inspiring teachings of one of the World's
greatest living Sages.
Paperback: 978-1-78279-729-6 ebook: 978-1-78279-728-9

On the Other Side of Love
A woman's unconventional journey towards wisdom
Muriel Maufroy
When life has lost all meaning, what do you do?
Paperback: 978-1-78535-281-2 ebook: 978-1-78535-282-9

Practicing A Course In Miracles
A translation of the Workbook in plain language, with
mentor's notes
Elizabeth A. Cronkhite
The practical second and third volumes of The Plain-Language
A Course In Miracles.
Paperback: 978-1-84694-403-1 ebook: 978-1-78099-072-9

Quantum Bliss
The Quantum Mechanics of Happiness, Abundance, and Health
George S. Mentz
Quantum Bliss is the breakthrough summary of success and
spirituality secrets that customers have been waiting for.
Paperback: 978-1-78535-203-4 ebook: 978-1-78535-204-1

The Upside Down Mountain
Mags MacKean
A must-read for anyone weary of chasing success and happiness
– one woman's inspirational journey swapping the uphill slog for
the downhill slope.
Paperback: 978-1-78535-171-6 ebook: 978-1-78535-172-3

Your Personal Tuning Fork
The Endocrine System
Deborah Bates
Discover your body's health secret, the endocrine system, and
'twang' your way to sustainable health!
Paperback: 978-1-84694-503-8 ebook: 978-1-78099-697-4

Readers of ebooks can buy or view any of these bestsellers by
clicking on the live link in the title. Most titles are published
in paperback and as an ebook. Paperbacks are available in
traditional bookshops. Both print and ebook formats are
available online.
Find more titles and sign up to our readers' newsletter at
http://www.johnhuntpublishing.com/mind-body-spirit
Follow us on Facebook at https://www.facebook.com/OBooks/
and Twitter at https://twitter.com/obooks